Intuitive Selling

A Practical, Holistic Approach to Sales and Marketing That Gets Results

by Thomas Wood-Young

Published by WY Publishing
15968 Longmeadow
Colorado Springs, CO 80921

Published 2000

Printed in the United States of America

Library of Congress Cataloging-in-Publication Data

Intuitive Selling / WY Publishing
       p.   cm.
       Includes bibliographical references and indexes.
       ISBN 0-9706233-0-5 (pbk.)
       1. Sales--Training. I. WY Publishing
       Library of Congress Catalog Card Number: 00-193135

Credits:
    Edited by Kinda S. Lenberg, Creative Liaisons, Fountain, Colo.
    Cover design by Bud Smoot, Creative Marketing Support, Monument, Colo.
    Text design by Kinda S. Lenberg, Creative Liaisons, Fountain, Colo.
    Printed by: C&M Press, Colorado Springs, Colo.

Intuitive Selling

A Practical, Holistic Approach to Sales and Marketing That Gets Results

What Others Are Saying About *Intuitive Selling...*

"This is a practical guide to being all you can be. I wish I had this book when I was a regional sales manager. It is a great teaching tool for managers. Sales techniques are out; building trust and developing relationships are in. People are more sophisticated today and selling techniques make people angry. This is a great selling guide for work and life. It's all-encompassing and each chapter is clear and to-the-point without a lot of fluff. This book will help you become successful."

David Kwessel
Sales Representative
Walter Company

"This book is great; I loved it! I'll read it again. It uplifted me and motivated me. The book pushed me to open up my own business and was an eye-opener. I passed it on to the rest of the team. They will read it and we will meet and discuss how we can learn from the book and improve our selling skills."

Jesse Carlson
Sales Representative
In-Sight Direct

"It was a sincere pleasure reading this excellent work. It covers a broad range of information in a very concise manner. Whether you are a seasoned sales professional, a sales rookie or simply contemplating entering the rewarding profession of sales, this book has a lot of meat for you to ingest. Tom Wood-Young has done an excellent job identifying a broad spectrum of external and internal life and sales skills possessed by the top producing sales pros. If you aspire to be more and make more in sales and life, you will find many of the key steps to getting these outlined for you in this book."

Jim Ander
President
Creative Profit Solutions

"As a successful salesperson who quit selling diamonds to establish consumer trust as an unbiased diamond expert, I believe in building trust as the cornerstone of sales. Customers don't buy your product, they buy you – what you are and what you believe. This book is important because it reveals the most important principle of successful selling: believe in what you sell and sell what you believe – the customer always knows. The sales profession thanks you."

Robert Hensley
President,
Diamond Hunters, Inc

"This is must reading for both new sales people and seasoned professionals. Tom Wood-Young has captured the essence of sales in the new millennium. This book has easy-to-read and to-implement concepts. Short chapters and concise action plans are ideal for the busy sales professional. *Intuitive Selling* is the "new wave." Technique selling is out! People today are much more informed and too intelligent to tolerate short-term relationships and inappropriate sales techniques. As Tom teaches, listening to the customer, suggesting solutions, creating win-win situations and developing long-term relationships based on trust and understanding are critical to continued success. I would recommend this book to anyone who is new to sales, in a sales slump or simply wishes continued sales education. YOU MUST READ THIS BOOK!!!"

Ron Barr
Sales Representative
The Alliance

"The book does a great job of demonstrating that being successful in a sales career requires skills that are drawn more from strength of character than of personality. I couldn't agree more. I think that salespeople of any age or experience level can benefit by reading this book. First, it can help reinforce one's sales career choice, as well as re-focus selling strategies and skills with the strength of character at the center. In addition, it can help familiarize them with techniques and available resources that provide a competitive advantage over the long term – such as the organizational and time-saving benefits of using contact management tools, for example. The book is easy to read and covers a broad range of practices, targeting ways to gain success in a career of sales. In fact, much of what Tom touched upon can be applied to success in any career – as all careers generally deal with meeting the needs of other people, groups, or departments.

Beth A. Harrison
Consultant, Online Marketing and Product Development

"I am a big fan of sales trainers and motivational speakers like Zig Ziglar, Tom Hopkins, and Anthony Robbins because of the way they simplify things and make them easy to understand and learn. *Intuitive Selling* ranks right up there with the selling pros! I found Tom Wood-Young's book so easy to read and understand. I wasn't bombarded with endless chapters of boring theory. Tom's book is filled with simple, easy-to-read chapters that gave me the motivation and confidence to come out of my comfort zone and to get in front of my clients and just do it! I would recommend this book to anyone who wants to make it in the world of sales. This book is a must read!"

Mark F. Mayer
Sales Representative
Colorado Information Technologies

"This book is loaded with practical methods, ideas and suggestions on how to increase sales by connecting with your customers in a realistic and honest fashion. Rather then using old-fashioned sales techniques that can be personally distasteful and financially counterproductive, Tom's tools allow one to feel good in the heart and also increase sales. You don't have to compromise yourself. I have used these methods successfully to significantly increase sales. I recommend this book to my staff because it works!"

Robert Rose
Sales Manager
MAPI

"Writing about potential and giving someone the skills to fully realize their potential are two entirely different things. On many levels, *Intuitive Selling* provides those skills and allows you to unlock the best of what is hidden inside you."

Kim Green
President
Advanced Therapy Institute

What Others Are Saying About Wood-Young Training Seminars...

"Your seminar was very helpful. After 20 years of selling, "role playing" still drives me nuts! With that said, I feel I learned more from your session than any others I have experienced in the past. Thanks for your help."

Bob Waropay
Midwest Region Manager
EAS

"Excellent seminar! I got more out of this one than one day with Brian Tracy!"

Better Business Bureau Seminar Participant

"Since taking the Sales Master course, just about every sales call that I have made has resulted in a sale. The training was very helpful, going beyond the nuts and bolts into the philosophy of selling."

Lorrie Todd
PageCafe Internet Consulting

"The course was powerful. I was on the edge of my seat. Tom is one of the best facilitators/trainers I have ever heard."

Uriah Werner
Allegra Print and Imaging

"I attended Tom's seminar, The Sales Master. Those who did not attend missed out on a very fine sales training course. I have been in sales for 15 years and I am always learning."

Leo Murray
Excel Communications

"The training is paying off for me big time. I have learned over time what is effective and what isn't. This training is the best money I've ever spent."

Doug Kysar
Kysar Machine Products Inc.

"The workshops helped understand how important hard work is and showed me how to better organize my time so I work better. I had my best two weeks in three-and-a-half years following Tom's training."

Ross Bradshaw
Investment Broker

"These are the best training seminars I have ever attended! They helped me realize that you have to love what you do to be successful. I especially enjoyed the discussions on the power of the subconscious."

Carla Wink
A.B. Hirschfeld Press

"I would highly recommend this training to anyone. Now I have to act on what I learned. The interaction from the audience was wonderful."

Kim Vaugn
First Colorado Mortgage

"The training covered all the bases and helped me understand the role of consultative selling and exposed me to new sales paradigms, as opposed to the old style. It was concise information and very motivating; I got a lot out of it."

Mark Thomas
Insurance Salesman
Primerica Financial Services

"The personal development section was very helpful. Successful sales people are aware of it and do something with it. Tom turns everything into a positive and does a good job."

Hank Perry
Independent Sales Representative
Nikken

"I enjoyed the motivational stories, and it helped me stay motivated and keep on going."

Heather Archuleta
President
Consumer Marketing Services

"Tom came up with new questions for me to ask – things I don't normally ask. He showed practical applications and how to put steps into action and how pre-qualification and research builds the closing ratios. Everyone was pleased and he did a good job."

Sheila Worth
Account Representative
John Wiley and Sons

"Tom's program motivated me to improve myself and go back to school and focus on my own professional development."

Lillian Blocker
Sales Representative
Moore Business Forms

"Tom helped me with my sales process and to keep my focus and stay level headed. I had great results right away. He helped me get many extra sales. Tom helped me feel more comfortable in meeting with customers and motivated me to go back to school and develop myself."

Juni Alexander
Market Specialist
John Wiley and Sons

Table of Contents

Acknowledgments

There are many people to whom I owe a great debt of gratitude. Writing a book is an enormous task that takes years of experience and countless hours to put the words down on paper in a way that makes sense and can be of use to readers. This book is the result of 20 years of life experiences and without the help of others, it would not be possible.

Thanks go out to my family, Pamela, Bryce and Blake, for their support and understanding during many days away from home and many hours on the computer. To Michael Corcoran for being my mentor and advising me with wonderful insights and deep knowledge. To Jack Day for teaching me invaluable lessons about sales, managing people and working in a corporate environment. To Kinda Lenberg, Val Faler, Dave Manofsky and Bud Smoot for working with me and helping to make the vision for this book a reality and to Josselynne Bippus for publishing my articles and seeing the potential benefits for her readers. Thanks to the editors of *Selling Power* magazine and many other fine magazines, newsletters and Internet portals that have carried my articles. Mike Pauly and Bob Rose for their encouragement and friendship. Keith Carter for emotional support and belief in my abilities.

Special thanks to my clients for their trust and confidence. Finally, to all the sales reps I have worked with, trained or managed, for their contribution to my learning about sales and the art of developing relationships with customers. This book is written for them and anyone who sells or markets a product or service on a personal level with their prospects and customers.

Introduction

The objective of *Intuitive Selling* is to help you sell more and enjoy the sales process. It is written for anyone who needs to develop a relationship with customers or prospects on a personal basis. This service to customers is the heart of selling. The only way this can happen is if you go out of your comfort zone and do things differently than you do them now. Some of the concepts and techniques you will read may make you feel uncomfortable or push you out of your comfort zone. This is a good thing! A key principle in selling, and life, is that you cannot increase your rewards unless you increase your value. You can only increase your value if you develop yourself through learning and changes in your behavior. This book is a tool to help make this happen. As you expand your comfort zone, you will broaden your sales.

As you develop these skills, they will become second-nature and part of your natural intuition about the sales process. To become a master of intuitive selling, you must learn to trust your instincts. This book was written to provide you with tools that give you the confidence to trust yourself.

If you follow the suggestions in this book, you will develop new skills and improve your sales abilities. This will enable you to bring more value to the marketplace. If you do this, you will gain higher rewards. This will not be easy to do; going out of your comfort zone is never easy. In selling, rewards come when you sell more and have fun doing it. Take action and modify your behavior; it will get you results.

Professional selling is a great career and business. Your performance determines your success and the financial rewards can be unlimited. This is not the case in many careers or jobs. Few careers provide such an opportunity to develop yourself, interact with a diverse group of people, learn about rapidly changing technologies, serve customers and understand the specifics of an industry or product line. Smart business owners have always understood the power of personal selling. No small business can get off the ground without a keen understanding of the sales process. *Intuitive Selling* will help you understand the sales process as it is happening today. There are no quick-fix techniques found within these pages. These lessons are hard work and include potentially huge rewards.

The concepts discussed are simple, but powerful. One sales rep referred to the ideas in this book as, "So simple they are genius."

The ideas of building trust with customers, probing to determine their needs, offering solutions and closing are core philosophies of this book. These chapters can become guidelines for you to follow as you develop a successful sales process. Re-read each section until it sinks in, making an indelible imprint and becoming incorporated into all of your sales work. Every sales position is unique, yet the principles apply to everyone. We are defined by our actions and our habits. Change your habits and you change your life.

This book is brief and to-the-point. The goal is not to overwhelm you with details, but to give you the basic, most critical skills in building effective relationships with prospects and customers. The chapters are short and easy to read. Time is money and it is critical that the time you put into this book pays significant dividends. I have found in working with thousands of sales people that too much information is overwhelming and results in very little proactive changes in their selling skills. Each chapter ends with critical action steps to help implement the sales skills discussed. If you do not take action on what you read, then you are wasting your time. Your sales habits determine your success and reading this book is an opportunity for you to change those habits.

Part I of the book reviews personal development, which is the foundation of improving your selling skills. Part II reviews the fundamentals of personal selling, including prospecting, qualifying, presenting, handling objections and closing. Part III discusses higher level selling approaches involved in building lifelong relationships with customers built on trust. Part IV discusses Internet marketing and sales issues, which play a critical role in sales success. Part V reviews future selling trends, how to develop a personal action plan and our sales training programs.

Take time to think about what you have read. Find ways to implement these ideas in your work. If you have questions, please email me directly and I will attempt to help you implement these ideas into your unique situation.

You can reach me at Tom@WoodYoungConsulting.com.

Thank you for purchasing *Intuitive Selling* and best wishes!

Thomas Wood-Young
September 2000

Part I:

Personal Development

Chapter 1

Do You Have What it Takes to be Successful in Sales?

So you are thinking about embarking on a new career and you wonder, "why not sales?" You like people, you tend to be outgoing, and your uncle Ted is in sales – and he makes a ton of money. How hard can it be? The answer may surprise you. As many as 30 percent of people who enter the sales field leave in their first year and only 20 percent earn 80 percent of the total compensation paid to sales reps across the country. Getting a sales job is easy; being successful in the position is very difficult. If you are willing to learn and develop the following traits, abilities and skills, then you may have the potential to be successful in sales.

Having worked with thousands of sales people as a sales manager, consultant and trainer, the following attributes have been demonstrated as keys to success in selling. Not all top performers have all these qualities, but many of them seem to be present in successful reps.

1. Understand the Value of Selling as a Profession

Sales is an honorable profession and one to be proud of. Without sales there would be no free market or economy as we know it today. Selling is the spark that drives our economic system. Top performers are not ashamed of being in sales and understand that their role is to help people. The word "sale" has its origins from the word "service."

2. Live With a Flexible Salary

Be prepared to set your own salary and have your pay be directly tied to your performance. Sales people are some of the highest paid people in the world, due to the nature of commission-based selling, with no ceilings and no floor. Very few of the top performers are working on salary. They realize that to reach high levels of success, their pay should be tied to how well they add value to their customers.

3. Leave Your Outgoing Personality at Home

One of the biggest mistakes people make in pursuing a sales career is taking a sales job because they get a charge from being around people. Outgoing people who love to talk and make new friends often burn out because of the rejection they experience and their inability to close sales because they are not listening. The best sales people are always listening, analyzing and asking questions so they can meet the needs of their customers. Relationship types can succeed in sales if they understand these laws and are able to deal with rejection by not taking it personally.

4. Learn to See Rejection as a Good Thing

There is so much rejection in sales, if taken personally, it will lead to unhappiness that will spill over into your personal life. Successful sales people see rejection as one step closer to a sale and a very powerful learning experience. They do not experience emotional side-effects from the loss of a sale. Rejection is a learning process and part of the selling cycle.

5. Become a Constant Learner

True sales people are not born, they are trained. There are no secrets or magic bullets that lead to success in selling. Successful sales people spend a portion of each day reading, listening to audio tapes and learning from the top sellers in their profession. You must become a full-time student and a constant learner to serve your customers effectively and stay ahead of your competition.

6. Believe in Your Product or Service

You must believe in your product and/or service with all your heart, soul, mind and body. If this is not possible, then do not sell that product or service. People will not buy from someone who does not believe 100 percent in what he or she is selling. This cannot be hidden; the customer will see through insincere intentions. One simply cannot effectively sell something one does not believe in.

7. Be Honest and Trustworthy

Customers want to buy from someone whom they can trust and who is honest. They want to buy from a friend. Learn to build relationships based on trust, honesty and integrity.

8. Learn Your Customer's Hot Buttons

Get inside the heads of your customers and learn why they buy. Push their hot buttons by meeting needs and adding value. This is where top performers excel and the most important area to be developed. It is the bottom line in sales.

Indeed, there are many more factors associated with sales success; however, these are eight of the most important. If you decide to pursue a sales career, utilize these traits and you are on the road to successful selling.

What is the Sales Manager Looking for in a Sales Rep?

If you are looking to get a job in sales, here are a few of the key areas that sales managers evaluate when selecting a new member for their sales team.

- A clone of the all-star sales people, or those in the top 20 percent who bring in 80 percent of the sales team's revenue.
- Commitment and loyalty to the company and product.
- A high degree of healthy competitiveness.
- Eagerness to earn high commissions.
- A proven track record in sales.
- Loyalty to the needs of the customer and an excellent listener.
- Goal-oriented individuals.
- Positive enthusiasm and a willingness to learn and grow on the job.

When interviewing for a sales job, ask the following questions:

- Can I see a job description?
- What is my compensation potential?
- What does your average performer make?
- What does your top seller make?
- How do I develop or find my leads?
- What is your average closing ratio?
- How much autonomy will I have?
- How many calls are expected per day or week?
- Is the job in the field or tele-sales?
- Can you explain the compensation plan?
- Who specifically is your target market?

These types of questions can help clarify the kind of sales job for which you have applied.

Action Steps:

1. How do you stack up against the eight areas mentioned above? Are there areas for improvement? Write down your thoughts on how you measure up in each area.

2. When interviewing for a sales position, be prepared and ask questions to ensure a good fit between you and your new employer.

3. What steps will you take to grow and/or improve in each area?

Chapter 2

Everything Starts With Attitude

T he most important decision we make in our lives is the attitude we choose to express each day when dealing either with people or circumstances. This critical choice determines success or failure in both sales and life. The key is the realization that we choose. That's right. You purposefully choose your attitude. Choosing a positive state of mind will lead to virtually unlimited success in your career – and your life. A negative attitude will lead to unhappiness, poor relationships, difficulty at work and ultimately, poor health. In fact, the most common causes of death in the United States are heart disease and cancer, which are related to stress. Stress is a result of a negative attitude, carried out via perceptions, choices and behaviors.

Where Does Attitude Come From?

One of the most powerful questions I ask during training sessions is: "Where does attitude come from?" Often the group will think collectively for a moment; many will respond with comments such as, "work," "people," "traffic" and other examples. Finally, a brave individual will announce, "Attitude comes from within us," which often leads to a chorus of "ah-has" as people begin to realize the power in that statement. You alone determine your attitude. We may blame others, circumstances or events for our situations; however, the key is our response to those things or people.

As you read this chapter, think about your day. We usually have a series of encounters with things and people that we feel cause a reaction in us. In reality, we choose that reaction – we have the power to respond in a positive or negative way to these challenges. Your challenge, especially in sales, is always to respond with a positive attitude.

Consequences of a Negative Attitude

Plainly stated, a sustained negative attitude will kill you. By far the worst side-effect of a bad attitude is stress and the top fatal diseases in this country are caused, in large part, by stress. Stress turns quickly into anxiety, depression and ulcers. Now that you know you have the power to choose, why choose negative attitudes? Sales people with negative attitudes struggle and have difficulty closing sales. One common statement coming from negative sales people is, "I'm not negative, I am realistic." This is an excuse for being negative. Reality is what you make it. Make it positive.

Rewards of a Positive Attitude

People like to be around positive people. In sales, customers like to buy from positive people who have confidence in what they are selling and help their customers enjoy the buying process. People do not want to be sold, yet they love to buy and own. Having a positive attitude will improve your relationships, make you happier and lead to success. The rewards of a positive attitude are enormous, if you are willing to keep your spirits up over the long-term.

Everything is a Learning Experience

Everything that happens to you in your life is a learning experience. This is positive. We may have hoped for a different outcome, but we must learn to face the facts in a positive light and move on. Let yourself become stronger from the experience, rather than weaker, full of doubt and stressed. Experience is a positive word for mistakes and the school of experience is one of the best teachers. Learn from these experiences by choosing a positive attitude that prepares you for the next challenge in life, which is right around the corner.

Avoid Negative People

One of the tragic results of a negative attitude is that misery loves company. Negative people will search out others and attempt to bring them down to their level. Indeed, this is how negative attitudes spread. Their negative influence feels powerful and they use it as a self-esteem boost. People do this in an attempt to feel better about themselves, but the end result is short-lived and unproductive. In sales, it is hard enough dealing with rejection from your prospects and customers. Find positive people and let their attitudes stick to you.

Being Positive is Not Easy

In my work as a sales manager and trainer, I have found that there are basically two kinds of people – those who take responsibility for their lives and those who blame others. People who take responsibility for their situations are positive people who see the world as a good place. They have made the conscious decision to be this way. This is not easy; however, understanding these basic principles about attitude is a major step. **First, keep in mind, choosing your mental attitude is the only thing you can control in your life.** Second, learn and practice a positive mental attitude and enjoy the rewards.

Action Steps:

1. Realize you pull your own strings and choose your attitude. The most powerful decision we make is all about our attitude. Make it positive.

2. Write down on a piece of paper three areas where you need to improve your attitude and make that change today. State specifically what your new attitude will be.

Chapter 3

Increase Rewards With Personal Development

In sales, as in life, there is a definite relationship between personal development and success. **The rewards you gain in sales are a direct result of the value you bring to your customers.** In other words, the more you give, the greater your rewards. The best way to increase your value and offer more is to develop yourself to the best of your abilities. Undeniably, this will add value to customers and increase your rewards. Ideally, this is your intention by reading this book.

Most sales people would like to earn more money, acquire material possessions and achieve a certain status. These things are fine and necessary. However, the key is to understand that you can only acquire these things in direct proportion to the value you bring to others through your service. Many sales people work extremely hard with the sole focus being earning more money. It's not about money! This will lead to frustration and financial worries. The focus should be on service, not rewards. The key to increasing your service is personal development. Following are some important steps in achieving effective personal development.

Gaining Rewards

As a sales person, you are providing a service. By developing yourself, you improve your service and increase the rewards returned to you. Often, the rewards are substantial and they include much more than money and status. They involve happiness, a greater sense of fulfillment, peace of mind, and better relationships. This is a form of inner success, which leads to outer success. Outer success can be expressed as increasing your value to customers. Before you can obtain success on the outside, you must first be a success within yourself. In essence, this is the reason for self-development.

People at their peak in the area of personal development experience life in a more positive light. They are more spontaneous and flexible; have lasting meaningful relationships; are focused; and produce extraordinary results. They have healthy immune systems and rarely get sick. In addition, they are balanced, confident, secure and know themselves completely on an inner level. They are consistently learning and enjoy life. These people are honest and trustworthy – and trusting of others – and are quite successful in business and other areas of life. If this is how you want to live your life, you must begin by changing and becoming what you seek.

Self-improvement occurs on these two levels: inner and social development. We can relate to the world by how we approach ourselves and others. The key to success in sales is to develop and work on your inner self first and let that work define how you interact with those around you. Unless you are sound in your own mind and body, you cannot effectively interact with others. This interaction leads to the greatest reward of all – meeting the needs of your customers.

Personal Leadership

You may not be a formal leader in an organization, but we are all personal leaders. Development of your internal leader is a must and occurs through self-improvement. Personal leadership is responsible for your mission and the attitude you choose. We are all self-employed, regardless of who signs our paycheck because we are the CEO of our own service business when we sell our services to an employer. In order to understand how to develop yourself to your full potential, you must write a personal mission statement and set goals. Find your true calling and define what success means to you. Your success is measured by how well you live your mission, goals and dreams. Be true to who you are and success will follow. Keep in mind, however, your service, as defined in your mission statement, should meet customer needs.

Work the Problem

Learning to work through problems is important in the delicate process of personal growth. Many people put self-imposed barriers in front of their development. Whenever you think the problem is outside, you are seeing things incorrectly. You must understand how you approach problems and be creative in that approach. Learn to manage and handle the problem, rather than having the problem manage you. Many times, the way we see the problem is actually the problem. Uncertainty begins in our thoughts and our attitudes. Do not let your thinking be your enemy; life in general and your thoughts in particular are not out to get you. The perceived problem is not the obstacle; rather, how you approach the problem is. This is defined in our approach to the problem and it is what we can control. Also, take the time to define the problem accurately. Charles Kettering was absolutely right when he said that "50 percent of solving a problem is accurately defining it."

Become a Balanced Person

Personal development is a process of growth and transformation that results in a more complete and balanced person. The rewards of remaining balanced are immense and include less stress in your life, better relationships, and improved health. To achieve balance, develop the mental, physical, emotional and spiritual parts of your life. The key is to spend time in each area in a balanced fashion. This is very powerful and has the effect of filling an empty tank with fuel. These four areas can be developed on both an inner and an external social level.

1. Mental

The mental aspect includes your mind, thoughts, and knowledge. Development in this area is achieved through challenging mental learning that pushes beyond your comfort zone. This includes reading, obtaining advanced degrees, attending seminars, engaging in stimulating conversation and other activities that constantly increase your knowledge base. People are notorious for lack of retention. It takes extra effort to force yourself to remember. Your mind is like a muscle; if you use it, it becomes stronger. This is especially true of memory and the retention of information.

2. Physical

The physical component is the body and its overall health. Physical development includes exercise, diet, adequate sleep and how you treat the human machine that is your body. Exercise is a must at least three or four times a week. There are so many exercise options available; pick something that you enjoy and will continue to do. Be a kid again and have fun moving your body and getting in shape. Find a training buddy or hire a personal trainer – but do something. Diets do not work. The body knows what foods are good and which to avoid. Follow a balanced diet, exercise and do not skip meals. There is no quick fix in staying healthy, except for heart bypass surgery. In addition, the body needs sleep to stay healthy. We know what is physically healthy and what is not. Choose only healthful options.

3. Emotional

Emotions need to be felt. In fact, repressed feelings lead to imbalance, poor health and inappropriate outbursts. Men are especially prone to the dangerous habit of suppressing feelings. Practice talking about your feelings with those whom you trust and keep a journal. Writing down your thoughts and feelings is an excellent way of expressing them. Emotions are a part of being human and we all have them, no matter how hard our exterior.

4. Spiritual

The spiritual component of your life should also receive attention. This includes asking profound questions about life. Find a way to search and develop a spiritual component in your life, which is not about religion or theology – it is about gathering a sense of why you are on this planet and asking big, deep questions.

Each of these areas should be nurtured, developed and maintained. One area should not be overused at the expense of another. As a matter of fact, the four work together in synergy. Balancing these four areas will result in maximizing your potential and reducing stress. When you are balanced, it is much easier to cope with difficult circumstances and life is far less stressful. The No. 1 and 2 killers in this country are heart disease and cancer. Stress is a major component of these killers. Maintaining balance in your life will help neutralize stress.

TV Creates Stress

Paying money to watch others live out their dreams is not personal development; rather, it is simply entertainment. Television, movies, and sporting events are designed to make money and serve no purpose in personal growth. A balance is needed here. Rather than live out our dreams, we watch others do it – and pay them for it! Enjoying a good movie, sporting event or TV show is fine occasionally, as long as you balance it with time for personal growth. Live your dreams; don't pay to watch others live out their dreams.

You Have the Power

There are several natural skills that we are born with that are used to balance the mental, spiritual, physical and emotional areas of our lives. These skills can manifest themselves during time spent alone or during interactions with others. Indeed, these uniquely human skills give us the power to choose our thoughts, emotions and attitudes.

First, we are self-aware. We can look at the past and look upon ourselves and our actions subjectively. We can examine ourselves and reflect on what has passed and what is happening in the present. We are able to listen to a deep, inner voice that sets personal direction and determines right from wrong. The best way to listen to this inner voice is to be quiet or meditate and let your mind be still. In this silence will come answers from our unconscious. Secondly, because we are self-aware, we have the power to choose. We do not have to accept our current situations; we can change of our on accord. Your situation does not define who you are; how you act in the situation does. Your own ability to make decisions and respond to your environment is based on who you are on the inside.

We can visualize the future and use our creative power to make our own future. The best way to predict your future is to visualize and create it yourself. Do not let circumstances create your future or determine your sale for the day, week or month. Make it happen today! Doing the right things will get you to the future you want.

Leave Your Comfort Zone

Professional development will improve your ability to handle the stress of today's changing business climate and maintain a professional life that is fulfilling and rewarding. Your first step in personal development is to take one. It is never too late – or too early – to begin changing and improving. If you are doing the same things you did last year, then you are not improving. In fact, you are falling behind the rest of those people in the marketplace. Staying the same is really falling behind as others progress beyond your abilities and add more value to customers. You must be willing to change to improve. Change is the mechanism of personal development and will feel uncomfortable. Learn to expand your comfort zone to include the things that once felt uncomfortable. Self-development will push you to new levels – and it is not easy. To get to a new place, you must travel a new path or road.

This learning process will take courage and require you to release any pride or preconceived ideas you may have about learning. Effective learning happens when you feel uncomfortable and challenged. The first step in overcoming difficulties is to admit to yourself that this will not be an easy process and realize that the rewards can be phenomenal. Learning is an ongoing process and applies to everyone. One of the great things about human nature is that we can always learn more. One word can be asked in regards to any situation: why?

Develop Your Skills of Observation

High-caliber sales people are very observant of the world around them and are quite familiar with their own abilities. They have developed a high level of observation, self-awareness and resourcefulness, which are the keys to finding solutions for customers. The ability to be resourceful can be developed through focus and attention on the world around you, away from your own thoughts. This helps you not only find opportunities that others miss, but also to become a valuable asset to your customers.

In developing yourself as a sales professional, it is important to know your limitations. This will enable you to determine where you need to adapt and change. Focus on the areas you can change and know what you cannot. Remember to surround yourself with people who can help fill those gaps.

Listen to other people's feedback, especially customers and co-workers. Take the time to see how you appear to them, not how you think you are coming across. The combined perceptions of these people make up reality, not your personal view of yourself.

Fear Stagnates Personal Growth

The biggest roadblock to personal development is fear and worry. Remove those from your mind. You will never be successful in any venture if fear or worry guide your actions. They often come in the form of excuses or self-created excuses for not changing. Do not spend time on what can go wrong; rather, keep your energies in positive, productive areas. When a negative thought enters your mind, use cognitive redirection and tell yourself to stop. Do not make excuses. Take responsibility for your thoughts and actions.

Live in the Moment

Live in the moment – it is the only time over which you have complete control. Do not live in the past and do not put too much emphasis on the future. It's fine to learn from the past and visualize your future, but take action in the moment. Remember that life is not fair and does not owe you anything. In fact, you owe life!

You are Your Thoughts

We are our thoughts, actions and habits. The beauty of being human is we can change our thoughts and habits. In fact, the only thing we can control is how we choose to respond to life. Learning and personal growth are perhaps the most powerful choices we can make. If this is how you want to live your life, you must begin by changing and becoming what you seek.

Open to All

Personal development and realizing your full potential is a life-long process, and at the same time, should be a matter of daily practice. We live in a turbulent time; "show me the money" is a slogan for many in a time of immediate gratification. Personal growth as a sales person is the most important step one can take. However, it is by no means limited to sales professionals. This is appropriate for anyone in business today. Any professional who interacts with others will have to practice a form of sales, however basic that interaction. In many ways, the very act of working with others is a component of selling, because fundamentally, selling is relationship building. It is based on shared value. There is little doubt that in today's competitive workplace, we are all part of the sales and marketing function.

Learn How to Sell

In today's business environment, knowledge is power, which leads to success and the key to personal development. This is absolutely critical in sales, where constant improvement is needed to remain competitive. It is important to know yourself, your customers and how to sell to them. The key is professional sales training. Millions of people are sales professionals, yet selling is not taught at most colleges or universities. Take it upon yourself to learn how to sell. Professional selling is a career choice and just as an attorney or doctor has a room full of books and materials to help them learn, so should the true sales professional. Learning the sales process is perhaps the most powerful choice you can make to develop your career. You are responsible for self-development, and, in turn, your level of success in sales.

Action Steps:

1. Every week put time into some activity that develops the mental, physical, emotional and spiritual parts of your life.

2. Make self-development a continuous part of your life. Expand your boundaries and your comfort zone.

3. Read a book, listen to tapes or do something each week that helps you better perform in sales or marketing.

Chapter 4

The Unconscious Mind and Intuitive Selling

In order to understand intuitive selling, it is necessary to understand the concept of the unconscious and the ego. These two parts of human consciousness determine much of our behavior, thoughts and attitudes. They are also important in understanding how we relate to others. They determine how we act on the surface and on a deeper level we cannot recognize consciously. Without getting too analytical, following is a brief description of the ego (conscious self) and the unconscious (inner self) and how they relate to your sales activities. Take time to explore this area further. It will bring tremendous value to your sales career.

Go Inside to the Unconscious

The first step to a better understanding of the outside world and knowing what success means to you is to get in touch with your inner self or the unconscious. The unconscious is the part of human beings that is intuitive. It is the power behind all human intentions and actions, providing us with dreams, creativity and imagination. It is who you really are at the core of your being and gives you purpose. Why do dreams seem so real? The mind does not know the difference. This is an expression of the power of the unconscious.

Your greatest challenge to becoming more intuitive in your selling and more successful in your career is to get in touch with the unconscious and listen to its direction. This will help you stay on target toward living your mission and goals and making the proper decisions as you respond to customers and the environment around you. The goals and mission are your internal compass, or steering wheel, in making daily and weekly decisions about your sales activities. As you make these decisions, step back, listen to your inner voice and keep them connected with your mission statement and goals. Trust the message of the unconscious; this is intuitive selling.

People may enjoy their work – some people are actually having more fun at work than play. However, most people would rather be doing something else. This is true because many people are not doing the work they love – or work they were meant to do (what their unconscious wants them to do). The unconscious needs a mission or goal. It can't wander, unless that is your goal or mission. Your greatest job in life is to find that mission and remove unwanted thoughts or things that are not true to that mission.

The Ego

We have a lot to learn from children and successful athletes. Young children have a high degree of contentment about them and the ability to bounce back from disappointment with ease, which comes from lack of ego. Also, anyone who has ever competed in sports knows that in order to function at the highest level of ability, he/she must get into the zone. Athletes must remove their egos and operate on instinct or intuition. They must operate from their unconscious.

The ego is the conscious mind. It is the voice in our heads that is critical or "parent-like." The ego is focused on rewarding itself and not helping others. It acts as a barrier to the pure messages that come from the unconscious. Thus, the terms "ego-maniac" or "big ego" are used to describe people who function solely from their egos. This type of functioning leads to imbalance and selfishness, two of the biggest barriers to selling success. You cannot possibly find ways to help customers and be a great listener if you are functioning from the ego. Self-discipline can contain the ego and quiet its voice. The concepts you will read about in this book, if put into practice, can help you move away from ego-centric behaviors, which ultimately leads to better intuitive skills and a closer connection to the core of who you are, which is in the unconscious.

The ego has a need to control and the false perception that things can be made safe through control. Let go of your need for control; it's too stressful and many times can lead to the opposite of the intended result. This leads to difficulties with change. The ego tends to fight change through fear and worry. The best way to deal with change is to realize that your unconscious is immutable. It is who you are.

Eliminate Negative Self-Talk

The ego is the creator of negative self-talk and fear. The unconscious listens to your self-talk and takes action on what it hears or sees. This is why it is so important to avoid negative people and events. Identify negative influences and remove yourself from them. Negative thoughts, images, and people hold you back from achieving your potential by influencing and programming your powerful unconscious. The unconscious needs only positive influences.

Find Quiet Time

Communicating with the powerful inner parts of your consciousness is difficult, but not impossible. The unconscious needs quiet time to work and express itself. Meditation, prayer or just sitting alone are excellent ways to quiet your mind and let thoughts emerge from your unconscious. This is not a quick-fix process and it takes time to develop the proper skills. There are many programs that can assist you in these areas and if used wisely and with discretion, can have positive results.

Perceptions are Reality

We see the world in two ways: the way we think things are and the through value we assign to those things. Work on changing your perception of how things are to produce big changes in your life. You create your own reality. Your unconscious is the key player in this. This is also true of your customers, who develop perceptions of you and your value to them and their organization. Being in tune with your unconscious is an excellent way of keeping your perceptions more clear and obtaining a better understanding of the perceptions others have of you.

Self-Image

How you see yourself equals the results you get in return. What is your self-image? Where is your internal barometer set? Picture yourself the way you want to be and set specific goals to improve your self-image. Determine and write down your specific goals and personal mission statement to be sent to your unconscious. These goals must be written down; if not, they will randomly move through your ego and conscious mind, rather then programming your unconscious mind.

Be around successful people, copy them and add your own personal touch, which improves what they do. Follow the advice of winners and do not just listen and do nothing. They are winners for a reason. Let go of your ego and take action on self-improvement based on what you have learned from winners. There is plenty of room at the top and success is lasting, otherwise it is not success.

This is a powerful boost to your self-image.

How would you act if there were no chance of failure? Act this way. Visualize your success and focus on the end results, or actions, you will be doing when success comes.

Remove limiting thoughts about success. Do not say, "I need to be"; rather, say, "I am this person." Visualize how you expect to be in the future and begin acting that way today. If sales is your profession, then realize that selling is extremely valuable and a service that helps people. It is fun, rewarding, and fulfilling to help others.

Action Steps:

1. Learn more about the ego and the unconscious.

2. Make time for quiet moments, with no interruptions, and let your mind be silent.

3. Listen to the messages about your life's purpose from your inner self.

4. Ask how you can create a personal mission that serves others (see Chapter 5).

5. Begin living this mission.

6. Learn to control the ego and to release your true inner self. This is the key to happiness and to developing intuitive selling abilities.

Mission Statements and Goal Setting: The Path to Selling Success

The first step on your road to success is to define it. This is accomplished by writing a professional mission statement.

A Road Map: The Mission Statement

A mission statement is like a rudder on a ship; it determines your direction. Without it, your purpose can be unclear, vague or prone to change-based external influences. A mission statement is a way of accepting personal responsibility for your life. We choose who we are, or want to be.

A mission statement should describe the key services and benefits you aspire to provide to your customers and explain who you are. Everything you do in your sales role should be in line with your mission statement. A mission statement is extremely powerful. The act of writing the elements of this vision moves your powerful unconscious into action. Research shows that we are many times more effective when we have a clear vision or mission.

Mission statements come from deep within us. Being in tune with this inner guide defines our values and uniqueness. A mission statement manifests this into action and brings greater meaning and purpose to work and life.

Road Signs: Goals

Goals help create a plan to allow you to live your mission statement. They should include career goals, financial objectives, sales goals, and all aspects of the sales process. Limit and focus your goals to a few key items that are most important. It is up to you to determine which areas are priorities, given the nature of your task at hand.

In order to obtain a goal, do not try to hold on too tightly to the desired outcome, as it will come across to others as desperation. Be able to let go, walk away, and not let your emotions keep you entrenched in something that will not produce a desired end result. Do not become too attached to anything. Too much attachment can lead to disappointment when things beyond your control do not happen the way you like.

When setting goals, ask the following questions: 1.) What is the end-result I am trying to achieve? 2.) How does the goal connect to my mission statement? 3.) How am I going to achieve this goal? 4.) How will I measure the results?

Mode of Transportation: Personal Action Plan

An action plan brings your mission statement and goals into reality. A mission statement and goals without an action plan are fantasy. The action plan makes the thought concrete and determines the action you are going to take to reach goals. In your action plan, focus on the practical applications needed to reach your goals and achieve your mission. Success does not come without focused action.

Many of us live with the imbalance of doing things that **need** to be done. These things are not necessarily important. We are trapped in putting out fires, meeting deadlines or managing our day-to-day work. This does not put you on track to achieving goals. Taking care of urgent matters will meet short-term needs and you will feel productive, but long-term growth and achievement are not present. Set goals and actions that are essential to reaching your mission – and do them.

Are We There Yet? Check Your Progress

Adopt a system that will move you to track the daily, weekly and monthly activities of your action plan. Begin each day by reviewing your schedule or plan for the day. Those items that are not accomplished should be carried over to the next day. Don't just wing it. Use common sense and keep focused on important areas. Prioritize these activities and set a time value to them. Evaluate whether you are staying true to your mission statement and on track to reach your goals. Change and improve the action plan as needed.

Arrive at Your Destination: Success

Have fun as you follow your mission and provide service to customers. When you love your work it stops being work and becomes enjoyment. Do not allow little things to get to you; most of what happens to us is a small occurrence in the big scheme of life. When obstacles come up, see them as challenges and learning experiences to overcome. We have the power to choose how we deal with them. Problems and obstacles make life a challenge and make rewards meaningful. Remember, all things will pass.

You are what you practice, think and do. You have the power to decide who you want to be by writing a mission statement and setting goals. A combination of living your mission statement and reaching your goals is the true meaning of success.

The Wood-Young Consulting mission statement reads as follows:

"Increase client revenues by providing sales and marketing training and consulting services."

Action Steps:

1. Read Stephen Covey's book, *The Seven Habits of Highly Successful People.*

2. Write a personal mission statement that outlines your service to prospects and customers.

Chapter 6

Time Management and Focus

There is a path that will provide you with success, goal fulfill-ment and many other rewards. It is your challenge, as a sales professional, to find the right path and set a clear direction. The key is proper time management. Ultimately, how you spend your time determines your rewards in sales. Choosing correctly is difficult and may be your greatest challenge; however, the rewards can be tremendous. Following are a few tips regarding keeping the proper focus and putting your time into activities that will lead to success.

Personal Mission Statement

As mentioned in Chapter 5, a personal mission defines success for you. Your mission defines the service you will provide to others, and is not limited to selling. Indeed, it encompasses all aspects of your life. The rewards you receive are in direct proportion to the amount of value you bring to your customers. This value is defined in your personal mission statement. It is your starting point and a reference for identifying the proper use of your time and setting goals.

Priorities

Every day we are faced with myriads of choices. They may come at us from many directions and seem overwhelming at times. However, we choose how we will respond to this stimulus and from them establish our priorities. For the most effective use of your time, focus on the priorities that you create and not your conditioned responses to life's situations. This requires you to realize that you pull your own strings and control your destiny. Most people can succeed in a variety of endeavors, yet fear usually drives them into a set pattern. Fear becomes the driving force behind setting priorities and the greatest limitation to success. Avoid this trap by realizing you can make it happen; your only limitations are the laws of nature and time.

Reflection

Reflection is the process of staying on track and maintaining focus. Monitor your use of time on a daily basis. Are you doing the things that will lead to success in your life? Are you living your mission statement? Intelligence can be defined as awareness. Reflection on effective time usage is a crucial aspect of self-awareness and is critical to proper time management. Are you making decisions based on fear or on what is in tune with your personal mission statement?

Find a Mentor

Find someone with whom you can talk about your goals and focus. A good mentor will not tell you what to do; rather, he/she will help you decide the proper direction or focus. Mentors see the world from an outside perspective and can help you with the reflection process by asking skillful questions. They also help you recognize limiting fears and help you find ways to move beyond irrational, obscure thinking and toward what is really important to you.

Make Use of Technology

Technology is a tool that helps us accomplish more in less time. Make use of technology to help you organize and accomplish priorities, as well as improve your efficiency. Technology is especially good at accomplishing many simple tasks quickly. This should give you more time to focus on important priorities. In sales, technology can become a competitive advantage. If you are not on top of technology, your competition will be.

Review your Focus

Re-evaluate goals and know when to change directions. There are times when your focus must change. This generally happens because of a change in the marketplace. Keeping abreast of changes in the market is a very smart thing to do. Indeed, accurately predicting the future of the marketplace is genius. We are capable of doing this if we focus on how we can better help people. This is the magic of your personal mission statement and your ability to change with the times.

Keep Balance in Your Life

Maintain a sense of balance in your life to help you better handle stress. As noted in Chapter 3, this is easily accomplished through constant, weekly attention to the four critical areas of self-development. Spend time developing the mental, physical, emotional and spiritual parts of who you are.

Action Steps:

1. Research and develop a time management system for you to use and get organized. You can only be as effective as your tools for managing your time.

2. Buy a scheduler for appointments, a contact management software system for call-backs and database management, and keep a separate to-do list for your weekly and daily activities. These three activities are the core of time management and should be separate from each other.

Chapter 7

Motivate Yourself to Success

Motivation is "an outward expression of an inward power." It is the inward power which incites one to action. Motivation is direction or focus toward a goal or mission that is fueled by energy and enthusiasm. It is the key to success in any venture. Motivation is like the motor in a car. The car is not moving unless the motor is running. Unless of course the car is coasting or being towed! True motivation comes when your own internal motor is driving you toward your goals, not when you are coasting or being pulled along by another's direction. Let's take a closer look at key aspects of personal motivation.

Motivation and Personal Leadership

True motivation comes from within. The highest levels of motivation come when we are in tune with our sense of mission. This is personal leadership. Our mission statement defines what we love and our purpose for being on this planet. When we are in touch with this true calling we are feeding and maximizing our motivation while functioning at our highest capacity. Without this true sense of purpose or mission, one cannot be fully motivated. The answer to motivational problems is personal leadership, or the deep belief in a vision of who you are becoming.

Maximum Production

Being in touch with your true calling unleashes a tremendous amount of energy that, when combined with focused direction, results in the highest levels of motivation. Three of the most important qualities of a highly motivated person are clarity, focus and persistence. The more clear the focus, the greater the energy to expend toward reaching your goals. Motivation encompasses visualizing success and moving toward it. Persistence is important because success takes time and many people simply give up too early.

Motivation in the Workplace

Very few people are highly motivated at work. In fact, most people work at only a small fraction of their actual capabilities. Imagine a workplace where everyone worked at even 80 percent of his or her potential! The key to being motivated at work is in understanding that it is not your employer's responsibility to motivate you. He/she can only create a motivational environment. **It is up to you to motivate yourself.**

Self-Improvement and Motivation

Self-improvement is one of the best motivators. Increasing your knowledge and learning new material pushes you beyond boundaries and brings greater rewards. Work to improve yourself every day and your motivation will increase. Allow yourself to expand beyond your safe and sacred paradigms.

The Personal Barometer

We all have a personal barometer that guides our comfort zone in response to our levels of success. Why do some people drive a

BMW™ and others a Geo™? It has to do with how they see themselves, as well as their sense of values. Any disharmony in this area will motivate actions to get back in balance or back into our comfort zone. Motivate yourself by raising your own personal barometer standards. Expect more from yourself and remove self-imposed limitations.

Positive Environment

It is very important to create an environment that motivates you. You should get a charge from where you work, not a drain. Also, the people with whom you interact affect your motivation tremendously. Spend time with those who build you up and support you – and definitely avoid negative people. If you don't receive positive feedback, do a personal assessment; there may be a reason for it.

Money Does Not Motivate

Beware of false motivation such as money. Money, as a motivator, is a very tricky proposition.   People adapt to the amount of money they are making and so motivation is short-lived. People work up to what they expect to be paid based on their personal barometer of what they are worth. When they reach that level, fixed pay adds no additional motivational value. Be careful that you do not place too much emphasis on money. **Your mission comes first and then the money will follow in direct proportion to the service you have provided.** The key is to provide the service that is your true calling.

Self-motivation is personal leadership via your own vision, goals, values and your own definition of success. A commitment to personal leadership with high levels of motivation is a long-term process. Undeniably, it will take time for behavior to change and be sustained – and longer for the rewards to come. But when they do, it will have been well worth it.

Action Steps:

1. Write down 10 things that motivate you. How do these motivators relate to your mission statement?

2. Where is your personal barometer set? Where do you limit yourself? Most of the limitations in life are self-created. Eliminate your self-imposed barometer and realize that the sky is the limit.

Chapter 8

Get Results From a Sales Coach

Throughout history, people have realized the importance of coaching and mentoring. In the early days of business, apprenticeships were the first step in developing a career and learning how to provide service to customers. Times have changed. Today, we tend to be thrown into our work with little or no training – especially in sales. This does not need to be the case. You can find a mentor, or sales coach, who can provide guidance and help you reach your goals. Your mentor can be a senior rep on your team, a trusted friend or a professional sales coach. He or she should have a successful track record in sales or coaching. Following are a few key reasons to work with a mentor or coach and how to go about doing it.

You Don't Have to Go it Alone

Successful athletes have coaches. They do this because they need someone who can look at their efforts from an outside perspective and suggest how they can improve. The coach works with them to reach their goals, and in some cases, may be the reason for making the goal. Sales coaching is similar to sports coaching in areas like teamwork, achieving goals, and being your best. However, it is not about competition or the concept of win/lose. The focus is on strengthening the salesperson's skills.

The Power of Personal Development

A coach helps you develop and grow. From this growth will come increased satisfaction and greater rewards. This is very important because it gives a more clear view of reality. Don't wait for circumstances to decide for you – develop yourself and move in the right direction. Coaches will not have all the right answers, but they will ask you the right questions. The answers to those questions are the keys to personal sales success.

Learn How to Reach Your Goals

Find a coach who has achieved some of the things you are working toward and ask him/her how it was done. Be willing to move out of your comfort zone and take action on what you hear. Your coach should be able to help you reach your goals. If you do not have goals, work with your mentor to set realistic ones that are challenging, rewarding and in tune with your values.

Accountability and Focus

Time management issues require focus on the things that will lead to success in our lives. A mentor can help you find and keep your focus. This is true because we are constantly faced with options and circumstances that force a decision. Many people make no decision, which results in more difficulties. A coach will help with focus and build accountability to your mission and goals.

Get Motivated

One of the greatest challenges to sales people is to maintain a positive attitude and stay motivated. A sales coach can become a source for this energy boost. Accountability to your coach is a powerful motivator. This can provide you with structure and help prioritize your activities.

A Sounding Board

A sales coach can provide a place to discuss things with honest feed-back and encouragement. It should be a safe place to experiment and try new ideas. No idea is a crazy idea, because creativity in sales is a key to productivity and success. Just as you are a great listener with cus-tomers and prospects, your sales coach will listen to you.

Give it Your Best

A good sales coach will ask you to do your best. If you are not doing your best, the coach will ask direct questions and remind you of your capabilities and potential. You may have homework and have to be ready to deal with straightforward requests and ques-tions. At the same time, your coach should know when to draw the line and back off.

Seek a Professional

Professional sales and business coaching is a major trend for the new millennium. We work in a knowledge-based economy and rewards are high to those who know their stuff. The bottom line is that an effective sales coach will help you become a greater asset in the marketplace and with that, reap greater rewards and meet your goals.

You may find the need to work with a professional sales coach. Professional coaching fees can vary tremendously and are usually dependent on how much total time is spent together. Most coaches working with individuals charge about $300 to $350 per month for one session per week. It all works about to about $100 or less per hour. Sessions can be held in-person or over the phone. The key to sales coaching is the return on your investment in increased sales for your business. Get a sales coach and discover an effective approach to personal and career development.

Action Steps:

1. Find someone whom you respect and ask that person to meet with you on a regular basis and mentor you. Most will be happy to do it. Act on the advice they give you.

2. If you have trouble finding a mentor, seek out a professional sales coach.

Part II:

The Art and Science
of Selling

Chapter 9

The Differences Between Marketing and Sales

Before we move ahead and review selling, let's review a few of the basic differences between marketing and sales. It is very interesting, in my work as a consultant, to hear how people interchange the terms sales and marketing. It is very common for sales people to refer to themselves as marketing representatives and for marketing managers to have no idea about the sales process and how it fits into their marketing efforts. Following is a basic summary of the very different roles of marketing and sales.

Marketing is the Big Picture

The marketing component is the single most important part of a business plan. It defines how customers will come to you and buy your products or services. It is a business-wide strategy that defines the target market, pricing, sales channels, the competitive advantage, market research objective, product/service, promotional plans and all other related functions. Personal selling is a component of the marketing plan.

Marketing Generates Leads

The primary role of marketing, in any business, is to communicate the message of the business to its target market and create inquiries, or leads. This is carried out in the promotional activities of the business such as advertising, direct mail, telemarketing, and the Internet, to name a few. This will drive potential customers into the first stage of the sales process – prospecting.

The Sales Process Generates Orders

The person inquiring will then begin the process of evaluating if this is the right place to have a specific need met. Usually, a sales representative will begin interacting with the prospect in a way that leads to a sale. In other cases, it may be a storefront, Web site or customer service rep that begins the sales process and takes the order.

Personal selling is the process of putting a human being in contact with prospects and allowing the relationship that develops to result in a sale for the business and satisfied customers. Marketing brings the prospects into the sales process.

Marketing Creates Perceptions

Marketing efforts create ideas in the mind of a prospect about how the company's products or services will meet his/her needs. This is an important step in motivating someone to inquire about the business or buy. Those perceptions should support the sales process and assist the sales representative in closing sales. Perception is reality in the mind of a prospect. This is called branding or public relations.

Sales People Fill a Need

The sales rep will then work with those perceptions and discover how to meet the needs of the prospect through personal interactions. This involves asking probing questions and listening, presenting information, properly handling objections and asking for the sale, or closing. This process is critical to business survival because it is the true expression of why a company exists, which is to meet the needs of its customers.

The Sales Strategy is part of the Marketing Plan

The sales process includes prospecting, qualifying, handling objections, presenting and closing. How this is performed is included in the sales strategy for the organization, which is a part of the overall marketing plan. The entire process must be linked together and supportive in each area.

Effective Sales and Marketing is Explosive

The absolute magic comes when sales and marketing efforts are coordinated and work together to generate results for your business. The most successful companies in business today have mastered this marketing and sales synergy and are reaping the profits. Work to coordinate and plan your marketing activities to create a source of inquiries that can be sold through your sales process. The process begins with a marketing plan. This is the ticket to great success in business.

Action Steps:

1. Understand your role in your business as a marketing professional, sales person or both. How do you contribute to the marketing plan of the business?

2. How is marketing different from sales in your organization? How does the marketing function support sales?

3. Describe your company's marketing.

Chapter 10

How to Develop a Marketing and Sales Plan That Works

The marketing plan is the driving force behind the success of any organization, no matter how large or small. Your marketing and sales efforts should be well-researched and planned in order to get results. The steps needed to hit sales goals are defined in the marketing plan. Before we examine the art and science of selling in more detail, the marketing plan needs attention. Following are key components of a successful marketing plan.

Identify the Target Market

The first – and most important – step is to identify the target market clearly. All the components of your marketing plan will relate back to the needs of the target market. Your business exists because of a specific market that will buy your products or services. This market needs to be identified in detail. One of the most common mistakes organizations make is to identify too broad a market and not focus on the specific needs of the targeted group. For your marketing plan to work you have to be able to answer the following questions:

- What are the needs of the target market?

- How does your company add value to that target market?

- What benefits do your customers receive from your products and services?

- Who are your current clients or customers?

- How can you find more prospects similar to your current customers?

Conduct Market Research

Market research identifies the specific needs of your market. Another critical mistake many companies make is to assume they know the needs of their customers and prospects. Nothing could be further from the truth. As sales and marketing professionals, we must constantly ask customers how to meet their needs better. Primary research such as questionnaires, surveys and focus groups can be used to gather data on the current status of your target market. Secondary research involves analyzing existing data. Use this data to develop a profile of your customer and gather general information about your target market. What are their demographics? Psychographics? Geographics? Buying habits? Why do they buy your products or services? How can market research be used to increase revenues? Do not make assumptions. Ask your customers the critical questions that will help you discover hot buttons.

Develop the Four P's: Product, Price, Promotion and Place

Reviewing how the four P's meet the needs of your target market is at the core of a successful marketing plan. They are at the key to defining how your marketing plan will work for you to generate sales. How do your products or services meet the needs of customers? Is there potential for new products and services to be developed? Are the products and services managed effectively? Is there a solid product mix?

Your pricing structure should maximize profits. Does your pricing structure maximize or impede your sales revenues? Are discounts used properly? What are your competitor's pricing strategies? Put in place a specific pricing strategy based on your target market.

Promotional efforts should be measured and provide financial returns. Establish a promotional mix strategy that will best reach your target market and result in increased sales. Is advertising actually generating sales? Can your advertising efforts be measured? How effective is your web site in generating sales? Is your sales force trained and motivated? Do they have good compensation based on results, and are targets and goals clearly spelled out? Evaluate how well you are performing in the areas of public and media relations, referral networks, word-of-mouth, customer service, direct mail, telemarketing and other forms of mass selling. How can those results be measured? How can results be improved? Your promotions communicate the message that explains how you can add value to your customers.

The place where your products and services are sold must conveniently meet the needs of your target market. Many excellent restaurants have failed because of location. Is your current location optimal for business? Are the proper sales channels in place? Take advantage of the Internet, the hottest marketing in tool in the last 50 years, to maximize you potential (see Section IV for details).

Gain a Competitive Edge

Finally, it is critical to determine your distinct competitive advantage. Who is the competition? How can your company gain a competitive edge? Has the competition been researched? How are you positioned in the market? You must be able to perform better than your competition in the eyes of your target market (see Chapter 32).

From each of these areas a sales and marketing action plan is developed. The critical steps that make the marketing plan a reality and lead to increase revenues are included in the action plan. Marketing involves intensive research, smart planning and a keen insight into the real needs of your target market. Develop a focused, well-researched strategy that positions you to maximize sales in your market.

Action Steps:

1. **If you have not already, take time to develop or review a marketing and sales plan for your business.**

2. **Enroll in marketing seminars and college–level courses to learn more about the science of marketing.**

Chapter 11

Prospecting: The Most Important Part of Selling

Selling may appear to be a simple process. However, it is actually very complex and extremely important. In fact, the sale of products and services is the driving force in any economy. Nothing happens until a sale is made. This is true of any company, large and small, or the government itself, which relies on tax revenues to operate. If there were no sales, there would be no taxes.

There are basic selling principles that can make the sales process effective and rewarding for both buyer and seller. Successful sales people develop and learn these approaches until they become instinctual. Each process has a strategy and focus, which we will discuss in more detail in coming chapters. The sales process is divided into four areas:

1. **Prospecting - Searching for potential customers.**

2. **Qualifying - Asking questions to determine interest and viability of a sale.**

3. **Presenting - Pitching services or products in a way that meets needs or adds value.**

4. **The Close - Get a commitment, write the order and conclude the sale.**

Selling is defined as a transaction that adds value to buyers by meeting their needs and results in mutual benefit for the seller and buyer. Prospecting is the focused, persistent and systematic method of developing sales leads and beginning relationships that eventually lead to sales. Prospecting can be carried out by sales people through direct contact and referrals, or through the efforts of the marketing department, which is responsible for generating leads for the sales staff. The key is to develop an effective prospecting strategy that begins the process of creating loyal customers. Prospects are the lifeblood of any business. As a result, it is imperative as a sales person that you become a perpetual prospector! Prospecting is to selling what breathing is to living – both are essential.

Know Your Marketplace and Identify Your Prospective Customers

The first step in prospecting is to identify your target market. Know the key hot buttons that stimulate action in your prospects. Establish a profile of your customers and determine why they buy. Do your homework and acquire in-depth knowledge of your target market. This is defined in the marketing plan and is critical to effective prospecting, which should focus on the prospects who are most likely to have a need for your products or services. Do not waste time prospecting into areas where you cannot provide value. This is why effective market research and a clear understanding of your current and future customers are so important. Focused prospecting will result in the best rewards for you and your customers.

Be Brief and To-the-Point When Cold Calling

First-time introductory calls, or cold calls, are usually needed to stimulate new business. Keep prospecting calls brief and to-the-point. More in-depth conversations will take place in later stages of the sales process. Know how much your time is worth. Time is more important than money because how you use your time determines how much money you make. Many times prospecting calls are a waste of time and it is better to focus marketing efforts on lead generation. One of the best groups to prospect to are inactive or dormant customers. These warm calls can be very effective in activating accounts and increasing sales. Never take for granted and ignore your dormant or inactive customers; they can be a gold mine for you because many have been waiting for your call.

Run the Numbers

The key to prospecting is persistence, because in many ways, prospecting is a numbers game. The more calls you make, the closer you are to a sale. Determine your conversion rates and use those to motivate you toward the next sale. Track prospecting numbers such as dials, decision-maker contacts, appointments and other activities. Each call brings you closer to a sale. You should be able to predict how many sales you will make for each 100 prospecting calls. Many sales people do not succeed simply because they do not talk to enough people. Successful sales people have large networks and are always busy with new prospects and customers.

The Impact of Fear

The biggest obstacle to prospecting is fear. Fear is a normal feeling, but should not be a barrier to your success. Fear, manifested via call reluctance, can be overcome through personal development, awareness of your fears and by changing your outlook. Try saying your fears out loud to people and see how irrelevant they can be. Fears are usually based on deep emotional issues and not often reality. Fear can be described as **F**alse **E**vidence **A**ppearing **R**eal. Fear can also lead to desperation. You should not want the sale so badly that you scare customers away. Prospects do not want to do business with sales people operating out of fear. (See Chapter 12 for more detailed information regarding dealing with fear.)

The First Impression

A first impression is usually made during prospecting. Although a first impression does not always make or break the sale, it is very important. Do not make up your mind about the prospect based on your first impression. However, make sure the customer's first impression of you is positive. You never know where the next big account will come from. Be clear about the impression you want to leave with people and ask those close to you what kind of impressions they think you leave with people.

Get Organized and Use Time Properly

Time management and organization are key to prospecting. One of the best ways to organize your prospecting time is to buy contact management software such as ACT! 2000™ or Goldmine™. The productivity increases of contact management software over paper are phenomenal. Because prospecting is a numbers game and requires quantity to work, time management is best handled with a technological solution. You must keep track of people you talk to and follow-up activities. This is best handled by technology, because you will more than likely need to meet many people. Disorganization will destroy prospecting efforts.

Set daily, weekly and monthly prospecting goals and stick to your schedule of calls and callbacks. There is no quick-fix solution – only hard work, persistence and commitment. Work your prospecting in blocks of two to three hours to avoid burnout. Take breaks to perform other sales functions. Find productive calling periods in your market. After three rounds of phone tag explore other options such as fax or email. Leave a message when appropriate on voicemail and let the prospect know you will be calling back. Constant, organized follow-up is critical. Include asking for referrals as part of your follow-up process.

Rejection

Dealing with rejection is part of prospecting. Be ready for it. Rejection is not about you. It is usually about the idea, product or service you are selling. Some prospects will not be interested, while others will. See rejection as part of the process and be ready to move on. You now have more information and you are one step closer to a sale. Learn from this information and improve your sales process. "No" is far better than "maybe," uncertainty or delaying tactics. Rejection gives you information and the best way to handle rejection is to make another prospecting call.

Prepare a Prospecting Script

It is essential to have a clear purpose or reason for calling in mind. A brief prospecting script can keep you focused and consistent. Improve the script over time to increase your conversion ratios. Practice and role-play scripts before you make a sales call. Avoid weak openers and have confidence that your message is important and will add value to the customer. Have a script prepared for voice-mail, screeners and decision-makers.

Networking

Personal selling is the process of meeting people and developing relationships with them that bring value to both parties. Networking is perhaps the best method to initiate this process. Networking is a social sales and marketing activity that results in meeting people, forging new relationships, discovering how you can help others, as well as building trust, referrals and sales. If done properly, it should be more effective than cold calling and a key to selling success. If done incorrectly, it will lead to frustration and few sales. Most people fail at networking because they expect too much too fast. Any relationship takes time and commitment for trust to be built and sales to happen. Be patient with your networking and realize that it is a long-term process. Remember that reputation travels and proper networking can lead to valuable referrals.

Networking can be very effective in group situations or one-on-one. The key is to have a strategy and work to develop the relationships and build trust. This has to happen before you can receive referrals or sales.

Following are a few key items to consider when networking:

- Set a networking strategy and attend functions that fit this strategy.
- Volunteer your time to organizations and clubs.
- Cultivate and develop meaningful relationships.
- Listen more than you speak.
- Be specific when asking for referrals.
- Do things that build trust (see Chapter 29).
- Set up follow-up meetings with qualified people where there is mutual benefit.
- Buy from people in your networking groups, without expecting return.
- Smile and be pleasant in your look and personality.
- Make networking a part of your prospecting plan.

Alliances and Partnerships

Partnerships and alliances are powerful, even those with your competitors. Finding the niche that is not being supplied by another company is a powerful way to prospect for new business. A perfect example is the real estate broker who refers to a mortgage lender. Find ways to partner with others and develop targeted lead sources. This should be a two-way street as you send interested referrals to your partner.

You increase your own wealth by bringing value to others. You cannot bring value to others unless you make contacts. Contacts are made through prospecting. If you do nothing else but prospect, you can achieve moderate success in sales.

Prospecting is like planting seeds and tending them with loving care until the harvest. You don't know which seeds will be the best or bear the most fruit, so you tend them all the same. Patience, persistence and proper technique lead to a great harvest.

Action Steps:

1. Prepare a prospecting plan, get very organized and set objectives for your prospecting. Make it a part of your marketing plan.

2. Identify and describe your ideal customer by looking at the current customer base.

3. Make a list of the groups that contain your ideal customer or have access to them. Visit these organizations, join those that are appropriate, form alliances with others and build a network.

4. Write an introductory prospecting script that clearly explains how you help customers.

5. Ask yourself this question: "Am I talking to enough people to reach my sales goals?" If the answer is no, then prospect more people.

Chapter 12

There is no Place for Fear

There is no place for fear in the sales process. You must remove fear if you are to reach high levels of success in business. This may be easier said then done, but it is your choice to make the change because you create fear. One common characteristic of the most successful people I have worked with is their ability to take risks and eliminate what others fear. Let's take a closer look at how to remove the self-imposed barrier to success – fear.

Fear is Learned

Children learn to fear the world around them from their parents and other stimulus. We are born fearless because we are born creative. Young children are full of make-believe adventures and creative play. As we become adults, the influences of others and the stress of everyday life forces the loss of much of this creative energy. In fact, many adults believe they are not creative at all – but this is simply not the case. Adults are very creative; we just use our creative energies differently than children. We often use our creativity to invent worry and fear. Ask the next person you meet a few of things they worry about and you are likely to get a long list of concerns and fears. Most of these fears are completely unfounded yet they can impact every decision and action he/she takes. There is no place for fear in sales – or business, for that matter. Let's review how to remove fear and worry from our lives and channel our creative energies into helping customers.

Understand Your Fear

The first step to eliminating fear is to understand it. This is not so easy, because many people tend to act on their thoughts without reviewing what they are actually thinking. However, awareness of your fears is the first step toward moving away from them. Fear and worry play a negative part in sales and approaching potential customers.

Call Reluctance

Sales people only spend about 10 percent of their time doing what earns their pay! This is usually because of fear of rejection. Review these numbers:

• 80 percent of sales come after five or more calls to same customer.

• 48 percent of all sales people make only one call per customer.

• 25 percent quit after the second call.

• Only 10 percent of all salespeople keep calling until they have a sale or a definite no.

Indeed, these 10 percent are the most successful and some of the highest paid people in the world. They have found ways to eliminate fear. Your challenge is to remove fear – especially from your prospecting efforts. The biggest obstacle to prospecting is fear, which usually expresses itself in procrastination and call reluctance. Fear is a normal feeling, but should not be a barrier to your success.

Remove Fear of Rejection

Your challenge is first to remove the fear of rejection. Negative responses from customers should not be internalized and affect your attitude. Keep moving forward and act like you know all your contacts will buy. This is easier said than done; however, always remember that you can choose your response to the actions of your prospects and customers.

Personal Development Reduces Fear

Confidence is very important in overcoming fear. One of the best ways to improve your confidence level is to develop yourself mentally, physically, spiritually and emotionally. This includes learning more about your product or service; gaining an understanding of your customers' needs; becoming a better listener; and constantly striving to improve your selling skills. It also includes self-development and personal growth.

Just Do It

The NIKE™ slogan "Just Do It"™ is in many ways pure genius. One of the best ways to get rid of fear is to do the thing you fear the most often enough so that the fear disappears. This takes courage. Successful people know this as a secret to success. Do not let fear become a barrier to your progress.

Change Your Self-Concept

You control your self-concept and attitude. Therefore, you are able to become a courageous person whose actions are not determined by fear, but rather a personal mission of service to others. The higher your self-concept the less fear you will have toward sales and in life. Working to improve your self-esteem and self-concept will reduce fear.

Talk About Fear

Say your fears out loud to people and see how irrelevant they can be. Fears are usually based on deep emotional issues and not often reality. A mentor, understanding manager or friend can help you realize fear for what it is and move beyond it. Fear can also lead to desperation. You should not want the sale so badly that you scare customers away. Prospects do not want to do business with sales people operating out of fear and they can sense it.

Action Steps:

1. Take out a piece of paper and write down all your selling fears.

2. Talk to people about these fears and realize they are the only limitations keeping you from succeeding and they are self-imposed barriers.

3. Begin removing these fears by doing what it is you fear and developing yourself more fully.

4. Avoid negative people and spend time with successful, positive winners.

5. Do things that build your self-esteem and confidence.

Chapter 13

Qualifying: The Art and Science of Selling

Prospecting was discussed at length in Chapter 11; now we move on to the second step in the four-step process – qualifying. The goal of qualifying is to determine why the prospect should buy. The best-qualified person to answer this question is your prospect, but this is not easy. People are not likely to give away their hot buttons, so you must qualify the sales potential of each contact. This is how you do it.

Ask Probing Questions

Create a list of probing questions which will help determine the level of interest in your product or service. Ask prospects about their work and the potential benefits of your relationship with them. Diagnose basic needs and explore options to meet those needs. Check out the budget, scheduling and time issues. Probe the amount of urgency. Ask where they get their information. Ask who makes spending and budget decisions. Make sure you are talking to the right person; if not, find the true decision-maker. Probe and intuit values and loyalties. Inquire about the past, present and future of the prospect and the organization. Find out what the customer does and find a way to help him/her do it better.

Keep in mind, if a prospect answers "no" to any of your questions, it could begin a downward spiral that may squelch the deal. Ask questions that get a "yes" response. Stay in the question mode, even if a prospect attempts to get you talking and do not waste valuable time on people who will not buy.

Practice the art and science of asking questions and probing to build trust by expressing to your customer that you are attempting to find ways to help. Often times, salespeople feel they are being pushy or aggressive by asking too many questions. They feel that being inquisitive is rude or intrusive. Nothing could be further from the truth; asking questions is the best way to show your customers that you have concern for them and their business and you are searching for ways to help them. This builds trust. The key is how you ask questions. Ask questions that show respect and concern for your customer. The answers will provide you with the hot buttons needed to qualify the need for your products or services properly. In the book *SPIN Selling*, author Neil Rackham discusses four types of questions to ask: situation, problem, implication and need-payoff. This excellent book reviews what the best sales people do when qualifying: the use of probing questions to determine how their product or services can best meet customer needs and add real value. Situation questions gather the facts and data; problem questions uncover the pain experienced by the prospect; implication questions determine the consequences of the pain; and need-payoff questions reveal how the product or services offered can add real benefit.

Find Ways to Add Value

People are interested in the value that you and your products or services can bring to their work and lives. They buy based on the benefits they receive from what you are selling. The buyer, not the seller, defines these benefits. Prospects will determine how well your products or services meet their personal needs, usually on an emotional level. It is very important to understand what you are really selling. You are selling how the customer feels after he/she buys the product or service. Probing questions and good listening skills will uncover this value.

Listen More Than You Talk

If you speak more than you listen, find a career other than sales. Qualifying should consist of 95 percent listening (or more) by the sales person. Control your emotions and focus on what the customers are saying. Keep them talking and listen to the hidden meaning behind the words. Empathetic, active listening is key. Take notes and repeat back what you think you heard. People love to talk about themselves and their company. They also love an attentive audience. This builds trust, a key to successful selling and rewarding relationships. In all parts of your life, let people talk about themselves and fight back the urge to jump in and talk about you. This will build strong relationships and lead to mutual benefit. This adds value!

The sales paradox is that you give of yourself in order to get back the sale. For example, give trust and receive trust in return. People will tell you how you can add value and close the sale if you listen more than you talk.

Get Inside the Prospect's Head

Get into the mind and thoughts of your prospect and out of your own mind. Focus on the needs of the client and how to add value. The goal is to be the person from whom customers want to hear and to help solve the customers' problems. If you do not understand where the customer is coming from, then ask. Stay focused on what is going on in the mind of your prospect.

The prospect is thinking, "Are you dependable, reliable, honest, and competent?" "Can you be trusted?" "Do I like you or do you like me?" "Do you know my business?" "Do I need these products or services?" "Things are fine the way they are." "I do not like change."

"What are the costs?" "How will this look to others?" Come up with ways to answer these questions before they are asked.

Selling is both an art and science. It is creative and analytical. Develop the qualities of the scientist and the artist as you qualify your prospects. Probe and explore like a scientist and listen and create solutions like the artist. This will lead to successful relationships with prospects and customers – relationships that result in sales.

Action Steps:

1. Write 25 or more probing questions to ask prospects and customers. Use these questions in your sales calls, even if they feel uncomfortable. Following are a few good probing questions: How do you see this moving forward? What are you looking to do? What are your greatest challenges and goals? What is your vision for your business? What is your budget and time frame? What is your level of commitment? Other than yourself, who are the key decision-makers? What do they do? What kind of obstacles are you facing? How can my product or service help you? Why is this important? How would that help? Where do you see returns? Would it be useful if...? Is there any other way this could help you? What kinds of benefits would you like to see?

2. Learn to be the best listener your customer has ever worked with. Make listening the key component of your sales activities.

3. Imagine that you are your customer. How would you like to be sold? Sell that way. Do a role-play and put yourself in the shoes of your customer, approaching the sales process from his/her perspective.

4. Read the book *SPIN Selling.*

Chapter 14

Why People Buy

Why do people buy? The answer may seem like common sense. However, most sales people have no idea why their customers really buy. They assume that customers buy for the same reasons the sales person would; in fact, the opposite is true. Customers buy for their own reasons, not for the reasons thought by the company or sales rep. You must understand why your customers buy your product or service in order to sell to them and meet their needs properly.

Emotions First

The root of any buying decision is based on an emotional response that is, in turn, based on perceived value or filling a need. This generally has no basis in logic or reason. There may be a certain amount of rationalizing after the purchase, but the actual decision to buy is almost always emotional. It is important to appeal to the emotions of your prospects and customers because this triggers their buying decision. People buy to feel good about what they bought and feel good about themselves.

Hot Buttons

Hot buttons are the emotional needs that, when pushed, result in a sale. In fact, people resist buying when their hot buttons are not identified. Hot buttons are unique to each person and are perceived differently by each customer, based on what will make him/her feel good or meet emotional needs. The master sales person will find out those real benefits and emotional needs and push the hot buttons that result in a sale. Hot buttons can range from how others will feel about the buying decision to the personal satisfaction of buying. People love to buy, because it meets specific needs. Those needs are hot buttons. Customers and prospects will resist communicating to you their hot buttons until enough trust is present. They do not want to feel vulnerable. People may love to buy, but they hate to be sold.

Choices Count

People have many options. Many times, the only factor that differentiates a product or service is what best appeals to the buyer's emotions. It is important to understand these emotional hot buttons and use them to develop a competitive advantage. The most important part of marketing and selling is gaining an understanding why your target market makes the choices it makes in purchasing your products or services. If this is not understood, then sales are probably going to competitors who do understand it.

Buying Signals

During the sales process, a client will communicate buying signals. The sales professional realizes that everything the customer does – or does not do – is a buying signal. Successful sales people can read and intuit these signals and use them as a profile of customer buying behavior. Customers do not communicate these buying signals directly until trust is at a high level.

Ask Customers Why They Buy

Engage customers in conversations that bring to the surface the mechanics of their buying process. In this way, the sales process becomes much more effective and focused on the core needs of the client. Go and ask your customers, "Why do you buy?" Address these issues directly and increase sales. Your customer or prospect is often thinking the following:

- Can I trust the sales person?
- I do not have time for this.
- I do not want to hurt the sales person's feelings.
- What are his or her motives and intentions?
- Is it safe to open up?
- Everything is okay the way it is now, why change?
- What will others think of this?
- There may be a problem, but what the sales person is offering is not the solution. I want to find my own solution.
- How can I postpone this?
- The sales person's solution is too risky.
- The benefits do not outweigh the risks.
- There is no solution to this problem.
- I am not convinced I need to buy.
- How can I buy?

Ask for the Sale

Finally, the sales master asks for the sale. Many sales people never ask for the sale because they don't think the customer wants to buy when, in fact, the customer is wondering, "How do I buy?" Remember, people buy based on benefits defined by them, not by their sales person. Understand this basic principle and better know your customers and how to meet their needs. Asking for the sale helps you understand why your customer buys – or does not. Remember they don't care to buy until they buy how much you care!

Action Steps:

1. Make it a point to ask each customer questions that will help uncover hot buttons.

2. Think like your customer, not your business. Walk a mile in their shoes.

3. Read the book *Why We Buy* by Paco Underhill.

Chapter 15

The Sales Presentation

A s first noted in Chapter 11, an effective sales process is comprised of prospecting, qualifying, presenting and closing. Prospecting is the task of finding new customers. Qualifying narrows your search to those most likely to buy. The sales presentation is your opportunity to present the key benefits of your product and service. This is where the spotlight shifts away from the customer to you. It is how you communicate to the customer the value he/she will receive from moving forward with the sale. This must be done briefly, because customers and prospects will not give you much of their time and attention. Customers usually have more important things to think about and their attention span will be limited.

The sales presentation can take many forms, ranging from formal, structured meetings with many visuals and props to casual, informal discussions. Following are a few critical components of a successful sales presentation.

Have a Clear Objective

Begin your presentation by clearly communicating your objective. This is critical; otherwise, people will form their own objectives. Your objective should always be centered on meeting customer needs and adding value. Focus on action not theory, and potential not possibilities. Get to the point and be brief. Organize your presentation and plan it extensively. The concepts should flow together well and key ideas should be grouped together. A presentation is the time for you to set a clear objective and present the solution.

Meet Customer Needs

The most important part of a winning presentation is that it meets the unique needs of the prospect. Those needs have been identified during the qualifying portion of the sales process. Focus on answering customer questions and communicating how your service or product will add value. This is based on the customer's definition of value, not yours. Facilitate the discussion so that you can continue to qualify. Keep the presentation interactive and dynamic. Use appropriate materials based on client needs and expectations.

Keep your ego out of the presentation. Remember the sale is not about you, it's about your service or product meeting customer needs and adding value. You are simply a tool to make this happen – however, a very important tool. Let go of expectations and focus on meeting customer needs and adding value.

Focus on Benefits and Adding Value

The presentation defines exactly how the prospect's life or business can be improved and how you can add value to both. Value is expressed in terms of benefits. People buy benefits that make sense to them. You should know your prospect's hot buttons and push them frequently throughout your presentation. The customer should be listening to you. Keep the customer focused by making the presentation personal, unique and targeted to the customer's needs. Request feedback and be honest and genuine. This will lead to trust and credibility.

Use the prospect's name at the right time and compliment him/her often. Use power words and relate to personal experiences of others and benefits they have received. Speak in the customer's language. Make ideas tangible by giving concrete examples of how your product or service can add value.

Be Prepared to Listen

Clear your mind as you listen to the customer and reiterate what he/she says to you. The time to be the best listener may be during your presentation. Do not resist their feedback. If a presentation begins to fall apart, be prepared to walk away. Do not compromise on your core principles or values to make a deal.

Objections During the Presentation

Objections will often arise during the presentation phase and this is normal. In fact, objections can be a good thing because they are an expression of interest. Don't panic and begin thinking you have come this far and now the deal could end. Remain calm and work through the objection process as you did during qualifying. (See Chapter 17 for tips regarding dealing with objections.)

Practice the Presentation

Rehearse and review your presentation until it becomes as natural as conversation. Do not wing it or come to the meeting unprepared – this could cost you the sale! Take the time to practice until the presentation flows with ease and confidence. Practice and preparation are the keys to presenting effectively. The best presenters are good because they have done it many, many times. The No. 1 fear of most people is public speaking – ranking even higher than death. The best way to eliminate this fear is do just do it.

The goal of the sales presentation is to meet the customer's needs and to put you in the position to close the sale. By following these guidelines effectively, the close will be a natural progression.

Action Steps:

1. The best way to practice a presentation is to speak to a live audience. Find opportunities to speak in front of groups at least once a week or more.

2. Write a 15- to 30-second description of how you add value to customers. You can call this your 30-second commercial and you should be able to deliver it at any time by memory. Remember, you only have about 30 seconds or less of your customer's attention. You must use this brief amount of time to make an impact. Focus on how you help, not how great you are.

Chapter 16

Closing the Sale

T he final step in the sales process is the close. Despite what you might have read or heard about sales, this step should be easy. quick and fun. It is the cumulative effect of all your hard work in the first three steps of prospecting, qualifying and presenting. If there is no sale at this point, then something was missed in the presentation or qualifying stages. The sale will happen only after you do your job effectively during the entire sales process. Following are the critical points to remember when closing a sale.

Ask for the Sale: Trial Closes

Always ask for the prospect's business. This is best done with trail closes and in honest discussions with the prospect. A trial close is the final qualifier that brings you a step closer to closing or determining the key concerns of the customer. An example of a trial close is, "Mr. Customer, are you ready to buy today?" or "Do you think we should go ahead and get started right away?" or "How does that sound so far?" Trial closes are usually questions that can be answered with a "yes" or "no." If the prospect responds with a "no," ask why. If the prospect says "yes," you have a sale.

It is important to ask for the sale at the appropriate time.

Attempting to close too early can put the client on the defensive and jeopardize your sale. For this reason, it is important for you to recognize where you are in the four-step selling process. Do not jump ahead. There should be no surprises at this point. Often times, the customer expects you to ask for his/her business and will wait for you to take the initiative. You should always ask for the sale following your presentation. In fact, you may have to use trial closes several times before the sale is finished. Following are a few good closing statements and trial closes:

- How does that sound? Are we on track?
- What is your time frame?
- How do you see the process moving forward?
- Are there other people we need to involve in this process?
- If we are to move forward, how do you see it happening?
- What is the budget for this purchase?
- Have you given any thought to how much this would cost?
- Can I get a commitment today?
- Would you like to go ahead and get started?
- What would it take to earn your business?

Do not make assumptions about whether or not a prospect or customer will buy. Many sales people struggle with closing because they assume that the prospect is not ready to buy, when, in fact, they are often times waiting to be asked. Present your trial close and then be quiet until it hurts and wait for the customer's response. The idea is to learn how you can help the prospect, not jump to conclusions and second-guess your prospect.

Closing Techniques Are a Thing of The Past

Forget closing "techniques." There is no substitute for the hard work that takes place in the sales process. Do not look for magic bullets or quick fixes. In fact, a prospect will see through these tactics and probably delay the sale or end the process altogether. If he/she is not ready to buy, you are not yet at the closing stage.

Follow the Four-Step Selling Process

The four-step sales process of prospecting, qualifying, presenting and closing should be learned and implemented until it becomes second nature. The key is to know which step of the sales process you are in and follow effective guidelines to reach your sales goals. Be aware that the four steps can become intertwined and mixed together during the sales process. (This is especially true of qualifying and presenting.)

Before you begin selling, carefully plan out your activities in each of the four areas. Prepare a checklist of information for each step. Target those prospects most likely to buy. Prepare a feature/benefits worksheet, script and set objectives for each step. Write down a list of probing questions and gather information to determine benefits that appeal to customers. Research and understand the prospect's business and related issues. Determine materials to use in presentations and practice your pitch. Be ready for objections and know your competitive advantage. Ask advice of your prospects and build a relationship with them. Cultivate even those brief conversations you may have and use these interactions to build your knowledge base.

Make Closing More Profitable

When possible, focus on selling high price-point products and services. It takes about the same amount of energy to sell high price-point products and services as it does to sell more inexpensive ones. Yet, the rewards are higher with more expensive products. Successful sales people usually sell high-ticket items. Low-priced items do not usually produce high rewards, unless sold in large quantities.

Many sales people never ask for the sale. Be the exception and always move toward closing by asking for the business, using trial closes and following the four-step selling process of prospecting, qualifying, presenting and closing. Lower-priced products and services require more assertive closing because they are short-term sales. More complex sales require more time and effort on qualifying and presenting.

Action Steps:

1. **Make closing a habit and be prepared to ask trial closes and ask for the business. Write down your trial closes and closing statements and use them.**

2. **Role-play closing until it becomes a habit. Do not attempt to guess if the customer will buy; rather, ask them to buy.**

3. **Determine your closing ratios by making a list of all the decision makers you talk to and tracking the percentage of people who actually buy.**

Chapter 17

Objections: A Natural Part of the Sales Process

D uring the sales process, prospects may express concerns or hesitations about buying. These are called objections and are a natural part of selling. It is best to practice objection prevention. Top sales people do this by focusing on providing solutions for their customers and prospects. If the customer can see the solution you are offering, then he/she has no – or very few – objections. The best sales people experience the fewest objections because they focus on value to the customer. Following are a few tips to help you handle objections.

Objection or Condition

The first step is to determine if it is an actual objection or a condition. A condition is a black and white factor that blocks the sale from moving forward. An example might be, "We have no budget." If this is true, than it may be a condition that cannot be overcome and your alternative is to follow up when there is a budget. However, test it first by handling it effectively as if it were an objection. In so doing, if you are unable to satisfy your prospect's specific concern, then it probably is a condition – a reason for not buying now that actually exists. An objection, on the other hand, is a request for more information and a gap that you need to fill in order for the sale to progress. Objections can be worked with; conditions are a dead end. Ask questions to determine if you are dealing with a condition or an objection like "Is that a condition to doing business with us?"

Validate the Objection

Always validate the objection and never argue or disagree with the prospect. Reiterate to the customer what you've heard and do not become emotionally attached to what is being said. This is especially important if the customer is becoming angry or frustrated. It is important to support the prospect's statement and clarify the objection before responding. Never respond to the objection immediately; rather, ask a question and give the emotional intensity time to diffuse. Often times, an objection may not be about the facts of the matter, but the emotions of the customer or prospect. You do not need to explain or be defensive. It is much more effective to listen and validate. This may be all you need to do for the objection to disappear.

Ask Questions

One of the best ways to deal with an objection is to ask a question. Understand that the prospect does not share your thoughts and feelings about the product or service that is being sold. In order to bridge this gap, use the words and thoughts of the customer and ask questions. The sales process evolves out of what is in the customer's mind.

Find the real concern and help solve the prospect's problem. The true meaning of most objections is not in the words themselves. The goal is to find the real reason for the objection. Treat objections as questions and uncover solutions. Work to develop a win-win situation. Ask for clarification, maintain good eye contact, monitor non-verbal messages and take responsibility for miscommunications.

Write Common Objections

Anticipate the most common objections you hear and be prepared to solve them with the prospect. Let the prospect know you have heard the objection before, but were still able to help other clients. Just as all other parts of the sales process, you must be prepared to handle objections. This includes making a list of all the objections you hear in your sales calls and having a strategy for responding appropriately to each one. What have you missed when you hear an objection?

Adapt to Ups and Downs

Remain focused and consistent in your sales efforts without responding to the highs and lows of the sales process. Be calm and collected when facing the loss of a sale or signing the biggest sale of your career. This is effortless selling, because it does not drain emotions or waste energy. It is effortless because you listen and learn from the customer the proper response and action. Objections may cause you to feel defensive or negative toward the prospect, or may stir other emotions within you. Your challenge is to remain level-headed and focused on the needs of the prospect, even if others are not. Do not emotionally engage in the objection.

Objections are Buying Signals

Everything the prospect does – or does not do – is a buying signal, including objections. Most buying signals are non-verbal. Understand that most of what is heard in a communication is non-verbal – even on the telephone. Successful sales people can read and intuit these signals. Understand what is going through the mind of the customer during the sales process. Engage prospects in areas that bring these thoughts to the surface. In this way, the sales process becomes much more effective and focused on the core needs of the prospect.

Price Objections

Price issues are one of the most common objections in sales. Remember price is a relative issue. The key is perceived value and return on investment. It is unwise to pay too much, but it is much worse to pay too little. When a buyer pays too much, he/she may lose a little money. When a prospect pays too little, he/she risks losing all value because of an inferior product or service.

The most important part of price objections is that you, the sales rep, believe that your product is priced properly. If you doubt this, then it will be very difficult for you to overcome price objections. In fact, you may want to consider selling something else if you cannot believe 100 percent in the price of your product or service. This is true of any objection. If you are concerned about the price of your product, remember that competitive pressures force prices down and it is the prospect who usually comes out on top.

Forget the Quick Fix

Never use sales techniques to handle objections. Customers can see a technique for what it is and are less likely to buy. Techniques bring up negative emotions and distrust. The root of any buying decision is based on an emotional response that is based on perceived value or filling a need. People may rationalize a decision to buy, but buying is determined on an emotional level. This is especially important to understand given the number of options buyers have. Many times, the only factor that differentiates a product or service is what appeals to the buyer's emotions.

Press Hot Buttons

People buy based on benefits defined by them, not by the sales person. Those benefits are perceived differently by each prospect based on what will make him/her feel good or meet emotional needs. The master sales person will find out those real benefits and emotional needs and push the hot buttons that result in a sale. Remember, people resist buying until their hot buttons are not identified. Objections and probing questions are perhaps the best ways of uncovering hot buttons.

Don't give up too early on the sale because of objections. Objections are good; they mean you are being taken seriously and you need to work toward resolution. See sales objections as part of the sales process and a request for more information. Find out what information they need and give it to them. This will result in satisfied customers and increased sales. Once again, do your homework and practice objection prevention.

Objections Reference Guide

One of the goals of this book is to help you better understand the sales process and put into action realistic steps and action plans that will help you reach your sales and marketing goals. The objections reference guide is a simple and extremely powerful way of handling objections. Study this guide and put it to use with your prospects and customers.

The first steps are to validate the objection, be prepared for objections and never engage emotionally. You then have three options for responding to the actual objection: ask a question, use feel, felt, found or inform gently.

1. Ask a Question

Your first option is to ask a question such as, "Can you tell me more?" "Would you mind expanding on that?" "How can I resolve the situation?" "Why is that?" or "How would you like to see it proceed?" These questions will help determine the real objection and uncover hot buttons. Validate the objection first and then ask a question.

2. Use the Feel, Felt, Found Method and Provide a Reference

This is one of the strongest messages you can communicate to your customer during the objection. It is taught in many selling seminars and may be recognized by your customer. Therefore, it is important that it is sincere and natural sounding when you use it. Following is an example; you fill in the blanks:

"I understand how you feel Mr./Mrs. Customer. That is a very valid point. Many of my clients have felt the same way. In fact, a customer of mine in _____ (state or city) had the same concern until he found how well _____ (fill in key benefit to this satisfied customer). You are welcome to call him/her for more information."

This approach is powerful, as it builds trust and leverages your satisfied customers to help do your selling. There is no better sales person then a satisfied customer.

3. Inform Gently

Sometimes objections arise because the customer or prospect is simply misinformed. You must be extremely careful in this area not to step on people's egos, because in their minds, they are correct. We are not in the business of making customers feel stupid. Therefore, it is very important to validate and inform gently. This may be a good time to refer them to your Web site for more information on the topic and learn for themselves. This is certainly more powerful than being corrected; it builds trust and removes the objection.

4. Use a Trial Close or Ask for the Sale

The final step in handling objections is to ask for the close. This may create an additional objection, which is good, or close the sale. You will never know unless you ask and be quiet while you wait for your prospect's response.

Objections Reference Guide

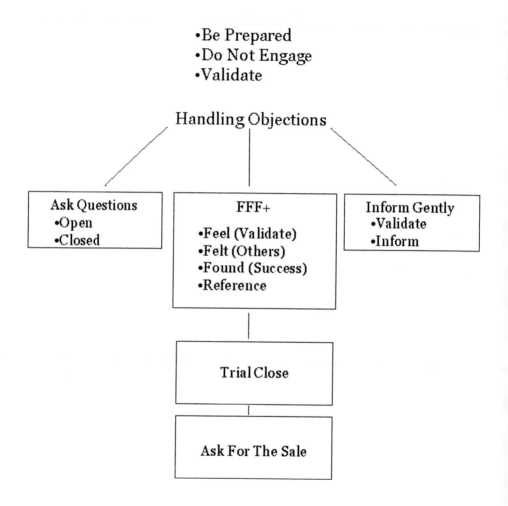

- Be Prepared
- Do Not Engage
- Validate

Handling Objections

Ask Questions
- Open
- Closed

FFF+
- Feel (Validate)
- Felt (Others)
- Found (Success)
- Reference

Inform Gently
- Validate
- Inform

Trial Close

Ask For The Sale

Using Feel, Felt, Found and Informing Gently

Following is an example of how to handle a common objection by asking questions using feel, felt, found and informing gently.

The customer may say, "You are too expensive," which is a common, price-based objection. Have questions prepared and ready to go for every common objection you hear. After you validate the objection you might ask, "How much do you expect to invest?" or "Tell me more. Have you received lower pricing at the same value from others?" Probe to find out more information about the objection and have your questions prepared.

Another option is to use feel, felt, found. "I understand what you are saying about price and that it is very important to find value in your purchases. Other customers of mine had the same concerns before they invested in our products. After they had a chance to see the value, they were very comfortable with the price. Here is a reference letter from a customer who initially had a concern about price." Show the prospect your letter and/or refer them to your satisfied customers.

The third option may be to inform gently. The customer may say, "You are too expensive." You might ask, "What are you expecting to pay?" The customer may give you a price that is simply incorrect. At this point, you must validate and inform gently. "I can understand how you thought the price was $95, but actually we are priced at $75." Always validate and inform gently.

This process will work with any objection and is very important in determining how you can meet the needs of your prospects.

Handling Objections

Following are a few of the most common objections heard by all sales people. How will you respond?

- I need to think about it.
- Please send me literature.
- It is too expensive.
- Your competition is better.
- We are happy with our current supplier.
- We have an in-house provider.
- We don't have the budget.
- Can you provide us with references?
- We are looking for more experience in this area.
- We are looking for a new, fresh approach.
- I have to talk it over with a few others.
- It is not what we are looking for at this time.
- It does not meet our specifications.
- I heard a few negative things about your product.
- You cannot meet our time frames and deadlines.
- We are concerned about your ability to follow up.

These are just a few common objections heard by anyone in sales. Be prepared, persistent and learn how to work with this natural part of selling and developing relationships built on trust. Handling objections effectively builds tremendous amounts of trust. Focus on the value you bring to customers rather than your personal needs. This will help you deal better with objections and rejections in sales, because it is not about you.

Action Steps:

1. Write down the 15 most common objections you hear.

2. Use the "Objections Reference Guide" (page 88) to set a planned response for each objection you hear.

3. Have a positive attitude about objections and practice objection prevention by focusing on your prospect's or client's needs and how you can add value.

Chapter 18

Twelve Ways to Increase
Word-of-Mouth Referrals

The most powerful form of marketing is word-of-mouth referrals. This is true regardless of the size of your company or
marketing budget. There is no better sales person then a satisfied customer. When generating referrals, your customers become
your sales force! Who better to promote your products than loyal
customers? Hollywood can spend $100 million to promote a movie,
but word of mouth will make or break the movie following its first
weekend. Following are 12 things you can do to help develop word-
of-mouth referrals for your business.

1. Ask for Referrals

The easiest way to generate referrals is also the most important.
People want to help others, especially when they know you are good at
what you do. Let your customers know that you are looking for referrals.
They will be happy to oblige and some will go out of their way to help.

2. Be Specific

Provide your referral sources with a few details about your target
market. If you are not specific in your request, referral sources have

the entire universe to think of and will generally not be able to think of anyone. Make your referral request specific. Keep in mind the characteristics of your target market and ask for referrals that fit those characteristics.

3. Align with Your Customer's Vision

Get inside the head of your customers and align with their vision. Be a resource who understands the needs of customers. Referrals will come when customers realize that you really do understand them and that your goal is to help, not just to make money and get the sale.

4. Develop Word-of-Mouth Marketing Promotions

MCI's™ "Friends and Family"℠ promotion was tremendously successful and built market share for the company that has been the key to their growth. Develop marketing promotions that encourage referrals and benefit your existing customers. Make the promotion worth your customer's time by offering valuable incentives for new referrals.

5. Promote Client Feedback

Ask your clients to evaluate your products and services and provide feedback regarding how you measure up. Share this data with current customers and new prospects. Obviously, correct the areas in which you are deficient and remove barriers to customer service. Include a customer survey on your Web site.

6. Continue Self-Development

Make your organization committed to constant learning. You must move out of the box and constantly grow and develop your knowledge and abilities or you will be left behind. Knowledge is powerful and people will come to you for expertise.

7. Build a Customer Community

Find ways to bring your customers together with other customers. This might be a chat room on your Web site or other customer events sponsored by your company. This brings a community of customers together and stimulates word-of-mouth referrals.

8. Communicate your Competitive Advantage

Understand why you are different from the competition and what sets you apart in the eyes of the customer. Communicate this message in your promotional activities. Be clear in delivering this message. It is the most important component of your direct marketing efforts and the reason people become loyal customers.

9. Listen

Become known as an excellent listener. This communicates that you care about others and builds enormous amounts of trust. The fact that you are the best listener the customer knows will be communicated to others and result in valuable referrals.

10. Build Alliances

Determine how you can reach your target market by developing win-win alliances and partnerships with other organizations. This is very common on the Internet as sites link to each other with great results. Look for organizations that currently service your target market and find ways to help each other.

11. Learn How to Network Properly

Take time to learn how to network effectively. Establish a networking plan and design ways to help others, which is the key to successful networking. Read and learn more about how to network effectively and go to lunch with a world-class networking professional and ask how he/she does it. The person will gladly share all the secrets because that is how one networks effectively.

12. Develop a Web Site that People Talk About

Establish a Web site that catches peoples' attention. When Web surfers come across a hot site, they typically tell others about it. It is very common to email web site links to friends. Find a way to make your site unique by adding value to your target market. This value is expressed in knowledge you can provide them to help improve their business operations or personal lives. (See Section IV for more detailed information about creating a Web site that works for your business.)

These are a few ways to build word-of-mouth referrals for your business. Remember there is no quick fix in sales and marketing and no substitute for excellent customer service and valuable products and services. Take the time to strengthen your marketing efforts in these areas and watch the referrals come pouring in.

Action Steps:

1. Establish a word-of-mouth strategy that builds trust and generates priceless referrals.

2. Set goals for your referrals and establish a word-of-mouth marketing campaign.

3. Think about generating referrals and you will begin working toward that goal.

Chapter 19

Selling on the Telephone

The telephone has become the sales professional's greatest tool. It meets customer needs and is cheaper and more effective than other forms of direct response marketing. Telemarketing is in a growth phase and is expanding as a sales outlet for companies small to large. Yet, many consumers and businesses are very vocal in their dislike for telemarketing. However, they overlook the fact that every year, millions of people are buying on the phone. The telephone should be a critical part of your sales process. Following are a few tips on how to sell and market your products and services effectively over the telephone.

Be Non-Threatening

In your phone presentations, be the person people would like to talk to and get to know better. Do this in your voice mail messages, especially with gatekeepers, screeners and decision-makers. The key is to listen and ask probing questions. Follow your customer's lead and be analytical or build rapport and establish a friendship-like conversation. This builds trust, which is essential to closing a sale. This process often begins on the telephone.

The First 15 Seconds

The first 15 seconds of your sales call are critical. In fact, the first 15 seconds can make or break the sale. Have a good opening that is sincere and catches attention without becoming a claim or boast. Questions can work in this area. Make a third party reference or follow-up on a mail piece, fax, email or ad.

Your first line must be powerful. Use phrases like, "we help businesses," "we offer," and "we provide." Explain how you can help, push hot buttons and have a sincere hook that adds value in the first 15 seconds of the call. Look to your mission statement for direction.

Get to the Point

Have a very clear objective and reason for your call. Telephone selling is a skill that requires simplicity and the ability to get to the bottom line fast. Selling on the phone is very direct and should hit to the heart of the matter very quickly. Time is money. Do not waste your time or your customer's time.

Non-Verbal is Powerful on the Phone

People often overlook the importance of non-verbal skills in telephone selling. Who you are, your motives and intentions will speak very loudly over the phone via your non-verbal skills. In some ways, this is the case even more than in a face-to-face meeting, where perceptions and appearance can be misleading or a distraction. Your focus should be on discovering the needs of your customers and working with them to determine how you can add value. Sell on the phone first and foremost because it better meets customer needs, not because you want to make money.

Keep Excellent Records and Be Organized

The volume of phone calls needed to be successful in tele-sales requires excellent organizational and time-management skills. Fortunately, contact management software such as ACT™ or Goldmine™ are excellent tools for tracking calls. Be very organized and track your telephone selling activities. Always return calls as soon as possible; this allows you to stand apart from the competition.

"Send Literature" Objection

One of the most common objections in telephone selling is the prospect asking you to send literature. Never send literature until you have qualified the prospect. Literature is almost always thrown out. Refer prospects to your Web site, fax or email information before you send information. Put more time into qualifying before you send literature, otherwise you will be filling the waste baskets of your prospects. Direct mail should be coordinated with telemarketing campaigns and sales people should use these mailings as a reason for the call. The "send literature" objection goes away because the materials have already been sent.

How to Deal with Gatekeepers

It is important to remember what screeners are paid to do. Basically, they have two functions: to protect their managers' time and to help people. When talking with gatekeepers, remember these two key areas. Build credibility and sound authoritative with gatekeepers. Sound like a CEO, not a sales rep. Express the benefits you will bring the boss. Convert the screener into an advocate for you because of the value you will bring to the company. This will also make the screener look good!

Be honest with screeners and ask them for help. Many will be happy to offer advice on how to get through and help you identify the decision-maker. They have been hired to help others. Ask a few brief questions; they have more calls to answer. Finally, if a difficult screener will not work with you, call before or after hours. Often times, the decision-maker will pick up the phone when the screener has left for the day.

Dealing with Voice Mail

Voice mail is the best – and the worst – thing to happen to sales people in the last 20 years. It is a fact of life in selling and must become a positive tool in your sales efforts. Remember trust is low in your first few contacts with customers. Prepare a voice mail presentation for your customers that clearly communicates how you can add value. Be professional, confident and honest. Do not use dishonest tactics such as bait and switch to lure people into returning your call. Most people will not return voice mail messages unless there is value. Leave a message that adds value. Do not call too often; once per week maximum is fine.

Do not wait for people to call you back. You should take the initiative and call them. A recent survey found that managers receive more than 200 communications every day in the workplace – and your voicemail message is only one of them. As a result, your call must add value. Let the client know you will be calling again in your message. Mention referrals or people whom you may know in common.

Keep accurate records and track how many calls are returned. Modify your scripts to maximize your returned calls. If voice mail does not work, try other options. Never give up because voice mail messages are not returned. Your best option is to speak directly with the decision-maker. Do not use voicemail as a crutch to reach your contact.

Prepare a Script

You must have a script to sell effectively on the phone. The script is not read word-for-word; rather, it is presented in a manner that consistently gets your message across. Do not wing it. Important items will be forgotten. Make a note of what works and use it again. Modify the script as you go. Focus on the direct value-added benefit of what you are selling.

Scripts are very important in the early stages of selling a new product or service. Over time, the information will flow more easily and the "script" will be memorized. Match your presentation to the mood and feel of the customer. Include in your script probing questions, trial closes and responses to objections.

Follow-up and Persistence are Key

Do not stop calling until you have a decision or people ask you not to call again. Telephone selling is a numbers game. The more calls you make the closer you are to the next sale. Prospecting is often best performed over the phone, and in today's competitive environment, there are times when it is necessary to make 100+ calls a day. If customers tell you this is a bad time, ask when it would be a good time and call back at that time. Ask for referrals from buyers and those who turn you down and do not take rejections personally. Never, ever give up. Many sales people fail because they give up too early or do not talk to enough people.

Proper Equipment

Headsets are essential to successful tele-sales work. In everyday conversation, most people do not speak with a hand to their ear or their shoulder pushed up into their neck, so why should we speak to customers in that manner on the phone? Invest in a quality headset and the proper equipment to work in a relaxed and efficient environment.

Practice Your Phone Skills

Tape yourself, role-play and analyze your speaking voice on the telephone. Can you build trust and confidence that will lead to a sale? How well do you listen on the phone? As it is in all parts of selling, the more you practice the better your success selling on the telephone.

How to Handle Tele-Sales Burnout

If you feel burnout coming, take a break. Pace yourself. Make calls in short spurts of 45 minutes to an hour. If a break doesn't work, then search within yourself, because professional selling may not be for you. In fact, telephone selling is not for everyone; however, successful sales people – and business people, for that matter – must be able to communicate effectively and sell their ideas or products over the phone.

Keep these suggestions in mind as you dial for dollars by meeting customer needs and adding value on the telephone.

Action Steps:

1. Write and implement a telephone sales strategy. Can you sell your product and service exclusively on the phone? If you can, then do it. This is a very cost-effective way to sell. Should the telephone be used to schedule appointments and follow-up on proposals? This combination of telephone selling and personal interviews can be very powerful. Should the phone be used exclusively to set appointments? Is it most effective to use a team selling approach with reps in the field and others selling on the phone? These are a few of the questions to answer in setting up your telephone sales strategies.

2. Write specific goals for your tele-sales process. How many calls per day should be made? How many decision makers should be contacted? What percentage of those decision makers should result in sales? Play the numbers game.

3. Set up the proper telephone sales environment, including headsets, contact management software, and scripts.

4. Budget your time appropriately to avoid telephone burnout and remain effective.

Chapter 20

Trade Show Marketing

Trade shows are a powerful method for marketing your product, generating leads and awareness of your company and closing sales. This is a fast growing part of marketing as more organizations realize the power of using a trade show to market directly to their prospects and customers. Your target market is physically with you in the same location for days at a time. This is a tremendous advantage for trade shows and will result in more growth in the future. Personal selling and effective marketing can provide big rewards in the growing trade show environment. Following are a few tips for developing an effective trade show marketing strategy and getting results.

Select Shows in Your Target Market

Research the proper shows to attend and set a budget. Get an idea of how strong the show will be and ask for references and show history. There are many resources on-line such as www.tsnn.com to help you schedule shows specific to your market.

Develop a Trade Show Strategy and Plan Properly

As with all business ventures, the first step is proper planning. It is common for larger shows to draw thousands of target customers to browse by your trade show booth. Just like any part of successful marketing, trade shows can be very lucrative, if done properly. Without the proper planning trade shows can be a waste of money and time. What do you hope to accomplish by attending the show and how will you make it happen?

A Trade Show Generates Leads

Lead generation is best accomplished by collecting names for sales follow-up. However, you must set up a system for collecting these names such as fishbowl give-aways or registration at the booth for an opportunity to be added to a mailing list. Make sure there are resources for follow-up upon your return to the office. It takes an average of only 1.4 personal calls to close a sale with an exhibition lead compared to 3.6 personal sales calls without one. Proper trade show follow-up is very rewarding.

Measure the Results

Review the returns against your total investment in the show. This helps you determine if the show was successful, which shows you should plan to attend next year.

Booth Design

Your trade show booth communicates your company's image. It is absolutely critical that you develop an outstanding design that works. It should be simple and clean, easy-to-read and complementary to other materials. You are attempting to draw people into the booth. The booth's design is their first impression of your business. Make it an impression that leads to sales. Visitors to a trade show booth make up their minds regarding how they feel about your display, your company, your products or services from 15 to 30 feet away, just by the impression the nonverbal messages your booth and staff communicate. Be selective regarding who works the booth and hire from the outside if needed. Avoid hiring models and temporary employees who are not trained in sales or who do not understand your products or services.

Use Effective Selling Techniques

Use the effective selling techniques of prospecting and qualifying to engage people and ask questions. Smile and listen warmly with genuine interest. Engage booth visitors with eye-to-eye contact and questions that open them up. Without this, your potential prospects will be talking with someone else.

Make Appointments

In order to meet with important, busy clients, it may be necessary to make appointments in advance of the show. This may get you the appointment with the busy prospect you have been hoping to meet. It can be a cost-effective way to schedule several important meetings all in one place.

Networking

Trade shows are a great networking tool. Visit other booths and network with attendees. This is a powerful way to begin new partnerships, alliances and perhaps discover new customers. Work the floor and do not be complacent and stay in your booth. Follow up with people you meet at trade shows; it may take several communications before you earn their trust.

Qualify

At your next trade show, identify your prospects' needs before you overload them with information. To find out all you can about the prospects who stop at your booth, shift your focus from showing and telling to asking questions and solving problems. Have two or three good opening questions prepared that lets the prospect feel comfortable and kick off the selling process. In fact, questions that allow the booth visitor to discuss why he/she is at the show and what he/she is looking to do are a good start. Move from these questions to more business-focused, probing questions that are part of the sales process. Remember the visitor should always talk more than you do. When prospects ask you a question, give them a thorough answer without rushing to ask them your next question. Your prospects should be doing most of the talking, but your questions shouldn't make them feel pressured or put on the spot. Keep presentations brief and focused on the prospect's specific needs.

Record Information

Even if you have a great memory, you'll need to make careful notes to remember critical information about each visitor. Design a customized lead card to help you gather qualifying information. Make the most of your information gathering efforts by having a system for analyzing and following up on each visitor. At the end of the show, you should have a completed lead card for everyone who visited the booth.

Organize Your Brief Presentation

With only a few minutes to probe, listen and react, your staffers have to organize their message differently. Find two or three key points that you want to communicate; they are most often your key benefits or competitive advantages. Then determine what facts can support those points. Choose the words and phrases that make the communication succinct and clear. Then practice it without committing it to memory.

Demonstrate Your Product

Hands-on demonstration is a powerful selling tool. If you conduct regular demonstrations, everyone who visits your booth has a chance to see your product in action firsthand. To take advantage of this opportunity, present your product's features, supported by the benefits that your earlier questions revealed are important to your visitors. Then ask questions that gauge their opinion of your product to keep them involved and to assess their level of interest.

When you're busy demonstrating your product, you won't be able to take notes on the answers you get, so it's a good idea to write down your visitors' names, then try to remember their comments during the demonstration and note them on the appropriate lead cards later.

Close on Action

Ask closing questions. Well-prepared closing questions bring the "presentation" to a close and prepare your visitors for follow-up. Perhaps more than any of your other questions, your closing questions will reveal just how serious your visitors are about buying. To capitalize on those who show the most interest, be sure to note your most promising prospects on your lead cards, or close the sale on the spot if you can. Questions about their buying process and time frame will help you identify your hottest prospects.

Long Hours

Trade shows are hard work and long hours. Be prepared to put in the time physically. It is not an opportunity to get away; rather, it is an intensive time to meet customers and prospects. Even though many shows are held in exotic locations, don't expect to see much more than your hotel room and the trade show display area.

Trade shows can get very busy. Your primary objective should be to help the people in front of you. No matter how eager you are to share the wonders of your product or service, you have to remember that to help your prospects, you need to learn about them. Once you let your prospects tell you what they need, you can tell them how you can help.

Action Steps:

1. **Establish a trade show marketing strategy as a part of your sales and marketing plan. Research the shows you wish to attend at least a year in advance and set specific goals for each show. What is your expected outcome from attending the trade show? How will you measure results? Set a budget for each trade show.**

2. **Design and develop a great looking trade show booth. Do not wing it. Your booth is the first impression and should build trust because it communicates professionalism and credibility.**

3. **Develop value with an added hook that brings visitors to your booth and generates excitement about your products or services.**

Chapter 21

Dealing With Time Wasters

Time is money. This is a basic principle and a law of selling. How you spend your time determines how you are rewarded. One of the sales professional's worst nightmares is the time-waster. These are prospects or customers who do not say "yes" or "no" to your offer, but rather delay or drag on the sales process and waste valuable time. Time spent with these individuals is like throwing money away. The difficulty is that many of these prospects seem to be seriously interested in buying and most sales reps realize they are time-wasters after it is too late and a large amount of valuable time is lost. Following are a few tips to help recognize time-wasters and how to deal with them.

Prospect Your Target Market

Prospect the right way and know your target market and its parameters. This helps you cover the bases and avoid time-wasters who are not in your market. It is important that you have an ideal customer profiled and you understand how to find more customers who fit that profile.

Qualify With Solid Questions

Be ready with solid, probing questions that help qualify the buyer, which may weed out the time-waster before you spend hours on follow-up and research. Ask the customer, "What would you do if you were in my shoes?" If possible, talk to others who know this prospect. Good, probing questions asked early in the sales process can help uncover a time-waster. If he/she asks for the same information repeatedly, he/she may be a time-waster and you need to probe and find out the true story.

A Time Waster Appears to be Too Easy

If there is a lack of meaningful discussion and very few concerns or objections, then this person could be a time-waster. As you focus on adding value, real concerns and objections come from prospects who are serious buyers and are looking to find ways to make the sale happen. Dealing with those concerns and finding ways to add value are a part of closing; if they are absent, it could be a red flag. If the sale seems to be too easy, it could be a time-waster. Do not be fooled into thinking that a lack of real, value-added discussions from your customer will result in an easy sale. It may happen occasionally, but don't rest your hopes on it.

Develop Your Intuition

Develop your intuitive abilities so you can read time-wasters before they misuse your valuable time. This is difficult to do; yet, the best sales people are excellent at this intuitive skill. Maintain balance in your life to reduce stress and help you give energy and attention to others. This helps you to be in tune and learn what people are thinking. Take time for yourself and develop the mental, spiritual, physical and emotional aspects of your life. High-level selling is a combination of understanding human psychology and developing intuitive abilities.

Give People a Way Out

Many time-wasters squander your time simply because they cannot say no or do not want to hurt your feelings. Give them an out and let them feel comfortable enough to say no. These people may seem to be too nice or are overly concerned about your feelings. The primary goal is too help people, not make a sale. If they do not need or want help, then it is time to move on to the next prospect.

The Authority to Buy

Often times, you may be wasting time with an individual who has no authority to buy. Probe carefully to determine if the sale is going nowhere. Ask questions about how purchases are made and who is involved in the buying decision. Attempt to determine who is the economic buyer (see Chapter 24) and meet with him or her. If access is denied, find out why. Your sale may be lost at that point – or you may have to change your approach.

Know When to Stop Selling

Professional sales people must know what they can and cannot control. This is why it so important for you to remain in control and know when to stop selling to a time-waster. Let the prospect know that you are ready to move forward when he/she is and the time for a decision is needed. Then move on to the next prospect. If you feel there still may be potential, then let the prospect know that you are putting him/her into your keep-in-touch program and you will be following up on a regular basis. The prospect will not feel pushed; rather, he/she will feel happy to know you will keep in touch for future possibilities.

Action Steps:

1. Develop intuitive abilities that help you learn to read people. Practice looking for subtle hints that define the true intentions of your customers and prospects. Review Chapter 4.

2. Realize that actions speak louder than words. What your prospect does and does not do is the real message that is being communicated.

3. Search out and work with people who will move on your initiatives and get things done and avoid time wasters.

4. Develop a method for staying in contact with prospects who may not be ready to move on your proposal. Contact them with value-added information that helps them do their jobs better or improves the quality of their lives. This could be a letter, email, newsletter, e-zine, phone call or other communication method.

Chapter 22

Negotiating: A Critical Selling Skill

An important part of developing business relationships and closing sales is your ability to negotiate an agreement or contract. The ability to negotiate is at the heart of any business transaction. There are many books written on the subject that go into great detail. Take the time to learn more about this important part of conducting business. Following are a few basic ideas regarding how to become a great negotiator.

Know When to Negotiate

The first step is to recognize when you are in a negotiation situation and when you are still in the sales process. Negotiating involves working together toward a mutually beneficial solution and assumes that the customer, or prospect, is in the process of buying. It is a way of completing the details and organizing the close. The sales process involves the steps that bring you to the negotiation.

Avoid Techniques

Recognize unprofessional negotiation techniques and tactics. This includes dishonesty, manipulation, threats, unprofessional conduct such as anger or swear words, stereotyping and other techniques. Call people on their use of inappropriate tactics and remove the technique's power. Learning materials may encourage you to use techniques, but be careful of the consequences. Do not use tactics in your negotiation; they simply do not build trust and may come back to get you. As in all parts of the sales process, the goal is to build trust. Any manipulation or technique will diminish trust. Stand apart from your competition and build trust by being honest, straightforward and focused on your customer's issues.

Do Your Homework

Your part of the negotiation process must be carefully planned. Know the boundaries on all issues and set clear priorities. Establish an objective and focus for each meeting. Build flexibility in your negotiation plan because it will need to change as you begin discussing options, conditions and the final terms. Do your negotiation homework and have in place a well thought-out strategy; otherwise, the results may disappoint you.

Understand the Players

If you could read the minds of the people on the other side of the table, your negotiations would be brief. Your challenge is to know the other side. This gives you a tremendous advantage and the ability to develop a true win-win situation. Ask prepared questions and probe to determine conditions and boundaries. Clarify responses and repeat the terms and conditions as you understand them. People negotiate based on emotions and want logical details specific to them. Uncover their hot buttons in these areas and save time and energy.

Find the Third Alternative

The term "win-win" has become a business buzz word and is probably overused because most people are still operating from the perspective of "win-lose," even though there are no winners in win-lose situations. Many times, true win-win agreements mean looking for a third option, or the choice neither party has yet presented. This takes work and creativity. Win-lose is really lose-lose in the long term. Find common ground and build on that to find alternative solutions. This is the magic in developing win-win solutions.

Remember "no" sometimes means "maybe"; ask for what you want and find the third alternative. You may need to ask people to submit another offer rather than continue to negotiate at a stalemate.

Negotiation Time

Skilled negotiators are masters of using time properly. Timing is critical in establishing a win-win. Take breaks and be very patient. Act as if time is on your side, whether it actually is or not. Gain knowledge and concessions from impatient negotiators. Set time frames and schedule the process to improve the negotiation and motivate people to action. If negotiations are moving slowly, suggest that they be postponed. This will provide good feedback on the exact position of the other side and give you valuable time for additional planning.

Give and Take

Start high and make concessions very slowly. This is a fundamental element of smart negotiations. Focus on individual issues, one at a time, and move toward consensus. Know your limits and probe to find the limits of the other party.

Be Prepared to Walk

It is often wise to walk away from a negotiation that is not progressing. It is a good idea never to place too much emphasis on a must-have agreement. It is better to have the flexibility and options to be able to leave an agreement on the table unsigned. This comfort level is self-created and when approached correctly, actually becomes your strongest negotiating advantage. It is the confidence that no matter what the other party decides, you will still move forward.

Action Steps:

1. **Train yourself to become a negotiations expert. Read books and listen to audio tapes in this area and learn more.**

2. **Make your negotiations focused on learning about the other party. This should be your priority in sales and negotiating.**

Chapter 23

Price and Value: The Direct Link to Your Bottom Line

Setting the correct pricing strategy for your products and services is a great challenge. This is true whether you are in sales, a business owner or at any level in the organization. Pricing has tremendous impact on your profits or commissions, because pricing not only determines the quantity sold, but also the direct contribution to your bottom line. Following are a few key points to consider when setting prices.

Set a Pricing Strategy

Start by setting pricing and profit margin goals. What is your target profit margin given your expenses? Determine if you are competing on price or quality. You cannot do both, because quality suffers when prices are lowered. If you are determined to be a low-cost leader, then efficiency in your operations is critical. On the other hand, if you are selling quality, then do not compromise on price. Discounts are a good strategy if you are a low-cost leader, but not when selling quality. Do not wing it. Use smart analytical tools to set proper pricing. Pricing correctly should not be based on intuition alone, but backed by smart market research. Put in place a specific pricing strategy based on the known expenses, desired profit margin, projected sales volume and perceived value offered to your target market. Do not make assumptions and be prepared to research and test alternatives. Are you pricing to generate volume and collect market share? Are you pricing to maximize profits? These are key questions to answer.

Maximize Profits

Your pricing structure should maximize profits. The price should be set so that profits are maximized based on the given demand relative to price. It is not uncommon for prices to be too low given demand. This results in lower profits. If prices are too high, not enough units may be sold as buyers are turned away. The key is to price correctly so units are sold and profits are maximized given demand. Does your pricing structure maximize or impede your sales revenues? Find the happy medium and profits are maximized. This is key to effective marketing. Remember a strong sales team can increase demand for products and services.

Do Pricing Homework

Review your expense budget and price your products and services accordingly. In determining a budget, keep in mind fixed and variable expenses. Review marketing expenses and how those are built into your pricing structure and marketing plan. Advertising, sales commissions, direct mail and other promotional activities are expensive and directly impact your pricing strategy. Review your competitor's pricing and attempt to determine their profit margin. Many businesses have very thin profit margins and others rely on debt. Have a clear plan for using debt wisely, or if you are fortunate enough, do not incur any debt.

Price to Gain a Competitive Edge

Make pricing a competitive advantage by providing more value than your competitors at relative prices. Research your competition and add value in a unique way that better meets the needs of your target market. Do this without increasing expenses tremendously and do what you do better than your competition. Price then becomes a non-issue in the short term.

Price to Meet Customer Needs

Get feedback from customers about your pricing. Customers are looking for fair pricing. People realize that they get what they pay for. The most important benefit is to receive a fair price for the value of the product or service. Price is equal to the relative value in the mind of the customer.

Prices are Being Driven Lower

Competition, excess inventories and the Internet are driving prices lower then ever before. Keep this in mind when setting your pricing strategy. We are all forced to do more with less. We have to compete smarter, focus on customer service and knowledge-based services. In these areas, our expertise and your customer's return on investment will determine a fair price.

Price and Value

It is very common to hear price objections from customers. Price objections are relative to perceived value in the product. Ask questions that get to the customer's key issues around pricing. Find ways to make your pricing add value and focus on return on investment.

Ask the following questions: "How much are you willing to

invest?" "Is price the biggest issue?" "How far apart are we?" "Is price your only concern?" "Do you have a budget?" "What were you thinking about spending for our product or service?" If you are selling on value and quality, let prospects know that you are not cheap and value is greater than price.

Believe In Your Prices

For those of you in sales, keep in mind that you must believe 100 percent in the pricing of your product or service. Any doubt in this area will lead to customer objections on price and a loss of sales. Customers will sense your lack of confidence. If you do have concerns about your organization's pricing, remember that the costs of running a business, market awareness and competition keep pricing reasonable. Have confidence in your pricing strategy and communicate that assurance to your customers. Your price should be equal to or even less than the value you bring customers. Follow these guidelines and be prepared for improved profits for your company and better sales commissions and/or incentives for the sales team.

Action Steps:

1. **Review your current pricing strategy and determine if it is maximizing your profits and/or increasing sales revenues. Do the research needed to set the proper pricing strategy.**

2. **Believe in the pricing of your products and services, or work for an organization whereby you can commit 100 percent confidence in its pricing.**

Chapter 24

The Complex Sale: Working With Buying Teams and Multiple Decision-Makers

Selling is often complex. Many times, relationships must be developed with a buying team or variety of individuals in a company. Many buying decisions are made based on the influence of this team. This leads to variations in buying motivators as each member of the team influences and impacts the buying decision. All the areas reviewed in this book apply to dealing with the complex sale; however, it is critical to understand the different players in a buying group and their motivations for buying.

An excellent resource for you to learn more about the complex sale is the book *The New Strategic Selling* by Stephen E. Heinman, Diane Sanchez and Tad Tuleja. In their book, the authors identify the four types of decision maker behaviors that make up the complex sale, as well as more strategic selling information. Individuals can exhibit different roles in different situations; however, your challenge is to identify their roles and modify your sales strategy to meet the needs of each decision maker. Following is a brief description of each area from the Heinman book.

Supportive Coach

The coach is the most supportive player in the sales process and usually the person who will introduce you to the company, set up appointments and give you a tour of the building. The coach sees the need for your service or product and is eager to get the program going. Coaches can be wonderful, but here is the catch: they cannot say "yes." The supportive coach usually does not have the authority or budget control to say "yes" to your proposal. If he/she did there would probably not be a complex sale because when the supportive coach is also the economic buyer, then your sale is almost a sure thing. This is a mixed blessing, as it is easy to get caught up in the spell of a supportive coach and the possibility that you will get the sale.

It is very important to qualify the coach and his or her buying power. In addition to qualifying the coach, you must lean on this person to open opportunities for you to do business with his/her organization. The coach will usually introduce you to the buying team and help you identify roles.

Economic Buyer

This buyer holds the purse strings and decides how money will be spent. The final approval or signature will come from this individual, as he/she has the highest level of approval for the sale. The economic buyer can play many roles in an organization, from very passive to highly involved. It is common for you never to meet this person face-to-face and it is very important that you know what makes him/her tick. The coach will be a great asset in this area.

Although any of these four buyers may make the final decision on your sale going through, the economic buyer carries the weight of financial authority and is very important in closing a sale.

The End-User

This person will actually use your product or service. The end-user is often the most quiet person involved in the sales process, but extremely important. Many companies do not include this buyer enough in the buying process, even though in many cases he/she is best adept at understanding the direct benefits of your product and service. Encourage conversations with the end-users and attempt to get them involved in your sales process. They are in a very good position to add value to your proposal, as they are usually looking for ways to save time, money and increase productivity.

Technical Buyer

The technical buyers provide the analysis of your offering. They are the "experts" on the buying team who provide feedback on your sales proposal. It is important to determine their degree of influence over the decision process and their concerns. Many of your more detailed objections will come from the technical buyer. Will they block the sale? If so, why? Do they support your proposal? Hopefully, they will approach your offer with little bias and review it objectively as it fits the needs of their business. This may not be the case, as personal and political influences impact their decision.

It is important to know how to speak their language. If it is over your head, it is a good idea to have someone from your company speak directly to the technical buyer in the terms he/she can connect with.

Understand the Buying Team

Make it a point to determine where your buying team contact fits in this complex sales process. After you have identified their roles, work hard to uncover their individual hot buttons through probing questions and your work with the coach. Remember multiple people can play multiple roles in this process. This will help you shorten the sales process and better qualify your customer or prospect. Develop a plan to work the complex sale and move the buying team toward a resolution.

Account-Based Selling

Complex sales usually involve account development responsibilities. The objective is to develop and foster a relationship that builds a healthy dependency, or partnering, between each party. This leads to steady revenue and the ability to grow your business as your account grows. This is the key to win-win account-based selling. You must be able to put in the time early on in the relationship that will nurture the seeds you are planting over time and lead to a bountiful harvest.

This will involve frequent communications, or cycle calls, to stay in touch and give you an opportunity to build trust. Find ways to understand the customer's business and become a partner in helping him/her grow and meet individual goals. The more you can do this with your accounts, the stronger your territory will become for your business.

Action Steps:

1. Make a list and profile of each member of the buying team and his/her influence on the sale.

2. Establish a list of probing questions for the coach, economic buyer, end-user and technical buyer. Use these questions to uncover hot buttons.

3. Read the book *The New Strategic Selling*.

4. Make regular calls on your accounts and find ways to make yourself a valuable asset with each communication.

5. Establish a territory sales plan and strategy by reviewing your A, B, C and D accounts and developing campaigns to present to these key accounts. Read more about territory management.

Part III:

Building Relationships and Trust

Chapter 25

Listening: Your Best Sales Tool

The most important skills you can develop are the ability to listen and understand how to add value to your customers and prospects. It is the key to understanding customers and the single most effective way to build trust. The first step to developing a relationship is to listen and understand your customers and prospects. Listening is also critical to self-development, as you must listen and understand before you can improve yourself. This is a high-level selling tool that is used by the top sales people. Although this may appear to be common sense, why is this particular skill lacking so much in today's business world? Becoming an excellent listener is not as easy as it sounds. There are entire books written on the subject of listening. Following are a few tips regarding the importance of becoming a great listener.

Be the Best Listener Your Customers Know

The best way to stand apart from the competition is to be the best listener your customers come in contact with. They may not realize it consciously, but your ability to listen and instill trust allows you to become someone who takes a genuine interest in and has a strong desire to help customers. Chances are your competitors are not excellent listeners. **This can become a critical competitive advantage for you.**

Listening is Hard Work

It takes emotional strength and discipline to listen. In fact, it goes against our natural instincts, which are to express our feelings and thoughts and relate our personal experiences to others. Simply put, most customers don't care about our personal views and opinions; rather, they want to know how you are going to help them and they want you to listen carefully to what they are saying. When you feel the strong urge to talk, don't do it. This is the time to be quiet and listen. If you do talk, repeat back what you think you heard to build clarity, especially in complex or confusing areas of your communication. This is very difficult for most people, especially extroverts. Listening is hard work that will definitely pay off in the long run.

Listening and Understanding Build Trust

Sales do not happen until a customer trusts you and your business enough to buy. Listening is a major key to building that trust and, in the end, customer loyalty. In fact, listening is a surefire way to build trust during a sales transaction. Many sales people are not trusted simply because they do not listen enough. Be an excellent listener and build trust. Imagine that your customer or prospect has an internal trust barometer. When trust is at high levels, the customers will open up and express their needs to you. If you can meet their needs, they will buy. This only happens when trust is high and the single most effective way to build trust is to listen and understand.

Act Like a Scientist and Use Probing Questions

Use probing questions to understand your customer and determine how you are going to add value. As we discussed, selling is both an art and science; in other words, it is creative and analytical. Develop the qualities of the scientist as you qualify your prospects.

Probe and explore like a scientist and listen and create solutions like an artist. Prepare your questions in advance and use them to direct the dialog and qualify your customer. Go into your sales calls ready to observe, take notes and get inside the customer's head.

Listen Like an Artist

Imagine that you are an artist searching for creative ways to help your customers. Create solutions by listening and determining how to help. Creativity will come when you are focused, listening to your prospect and listening to your intuition. It is the combination of the scientist and the artist that makes a great listener and a top-level sales person.

Customers May Not Open Up

Customers will not tell you everything you need to know unless they trust you. They do not want to be seen as vulnerable and have you take advantage of them. Listening is the key to solving this problem. Your challenge is to move them from the fear of loss to the desire for gain, which is done through building trust by providing benefits and meeting their needs. Listening helps you find ways to add value. It also helps you gather valuable feedback on your products and/or services. This is feedback that will only surface if trust is present. Customers do not want conflict or to hurt your feelings. They will not provide constructive feedback unless they can trust your response. Build trust through listening and observe your customers as they communicate more honestly with you.

Silence is Okay

Many sales people talk because they feel silence is uncomfortable when, in fact, magic can happen in silence. During a silent period, your prospect or customer is often thinking of a question or pondering his/her next move. Let the person think and understand that silence is okay. It is especially important to be quiet after you ask for their business. Let the customer be the first to speak and you probably have a sale.

Get Inside the Heads of Your Customers

Determine your customers' "hot buttons" or the specific things that will cause them to buy. Listening allows you to get inside the heads of your customers and understand their particular hot buttons. You will then be better equipped to determine how you can add value to their busy lives. Always remember to listen more than you talk and you will develop a strong competitive advantage by becoming an incredible listener.

Action Steps:

1. **In your next sales call, observe who does most of the talking.**

2. **Make it your goal to be the best listener your customers or prospects know.**

3. **Practice listening and relating back to others what you think you understand.**

Chapter 26

Customer Relationships: The Key to Sales Prosperity

S elling is the process of building a trusting relationship with people. This should not be a passing trend or sales technique, but a way of life. The relationships you develop with customers determine your level of sales success. Following are a few suggestions regarding how to make this happen.

Build Better Relationships by Improving Yourself

The first step in building effective relationships is to take a good, hard look at yourself. Where can you improve to become a greater asset to your target market? You cannot change or control your customers, but you can choose how you interact with them. This is the key to building effective relationships. Your relationships with others are a reflection of how you feel about yourself. If you are a positive person, then you are more likely to find others positive. If you like who you are, you are more likely to like others. This is why self-development is so important to improved relationships. It is an excellent way to improve your self-concept and reduce fear. Fear leads to distrust of others and weakens relationships. An improved self-concept leads to confidence, stronger relationships and greater sales success.

Build a Partnership

Think of yourself as a partner aligned with the customer. The goal is service to the customer and the customer's clients. Ask yourself this question: "How can I help my customers and their customers improve and grow their businesses or improve the quality of their lives?" Develop a healthy sales dependency verses short-term quick in-and-out approaches. Develop a customer rather than a sale. People want to develop a relationship with someone who is dependable and meets their needs. In this way, the relationship becomes more important than the product or service. The relationship actually becomes your competitive advantage and a real benefit to the customer. Indeed, the customer buys you as much, if not more, than the actual product or service. This gives tremendous importance to your relationships with your customers and prospects. This is the power in personal selling.

Build Trust

Trust is the glue that holds the sales person/customer relationship together. Trust is expressed repeatedly in your actions – simple things such as returning phone calls immediately or doing exactly what you say you will do. In this way, trust is an absolutely essential part of sales. If trust is not present, customers will not buy.

Trust is built by showing competence and credibility. Competence is getting the job done right – better than competitors. Credibility is your character, integrity and honesty. Your competence is expressed through knowledge of the client's needs and the ability to work with others. Your character should be composed of an abundance mentality that is expressed through giving and unselfish behavior. High character traits lead to strong credibility.

Trust is also built through frequent communications and listening to customer issues. Listening builds trust because it shows how much you value the customer. Contact customers on a regular basis and make use of check-in, cycle, and new product announcement calls. Inquire about the needs and thoughts of customers and listen to their response. Other ways to build trust include:

- Listen, listen, listen and then listen more.
- Return all phone calls immediately.
- Send thank-you notes.
- Do something different and special; be creative.
- Handle complaints promptly with empathy and honesty.
- Be extremely dependable and organized.
- Offer great customer service.
- Show sincere appreciation.
- Value customers; they pay our salaries.

Do these things because people want to feel special and valued. More importantly, do these things without any expectation of return from the customer. Understand that if you give one, you will be rewarded with 10. Trust will be discussed more in Chapter 29.

Build Relationships with all Types

You cannot please everyone. However, remain objective and build relationships with many different personality types. The goal is to allow people to be who they are and to understand them – not to attempt to criticize or correct them. When a challenging customer comes along, spend more time listening with empathy and working toward a win-win. This is done without compromising your key principles, values or mission. Improve your self-concept and it becomes easier to relate to all types of people.

Build Relationships by Adding Value

Find ways to become a valuable resource to the client. Identify the core problem, not the symptom, and create solutions that add value to customers. In fact, guide customers through the value-added learning process. They may need to learn how your product or service can add value. Know that people learn differently and retain what they understand and have interest in. People are very interested in what will add value to them.

Be creative and flexible in your relationships with people. Know the difference between fact, opinion and assumption and recognize bias and emotion. Be the person customers want to see and meet with because you add direct value in the form of a productive and effective relationship. Then there is mutual benefit, respect and appreciation.

Action Steps:

1. Perform a self-evaluation of how you develop relationships. Do you have high-quality friends and associates where trust is present?

2. Do you see the world as a positive place where people are trustworthy and honest? Or do you see the world as a negative place and most people are not to be trusted? How you answer these questions determines your potential for effective sales relationships.

3. Finds ways to improve who you are and become a better person. Become the type of person that people want to be around. Do this by maintaining high self-confidence levels and a very positive self-concept.

Chapter 27

Personality Preferences in Sales

Your personality is a strong component of your business success. It is even more critical to your success in developing relationships, building trust and selling more effectively. Why is so much emphasis put on personalities in business? Should it not be focused on results and effectiveness? Perhaps in theory, but in real life, people are emotional beings with feelings and sensitivities to others. These emotions are so powerful in determining our actions that personalities become a major factor in our sales effectiveness with customers and relationships in general. Therefore, personalities play a big role in marketing and business success.

Once again, you pull your own strings and control your emotional responses. Because of this, you can also control your personality. It is not easy. We all have personality preferences that keep us in our comfort zones. Your challenge is to develop the type of personality that is compatible with many personality types. This is a key step to creating win-win sales relationships.

Let's take a look at personalities in more detail. As you read this chapter, try to determine your own personality profile. Knowing your own personality preferences is important in understanding personalities that you like and those that you dislike.

Myers-Briggs

C.G. Jung first suggested theories of personality in the early 1930s to describe human behavior. His work was modified and eventually developed into the Myers-Briggs testing instrument to determine personality preferences. It is one of the most common testing instruments in the world. The Myers-Briggs program is an excellent method for understanding personalities and taking the test is highly recommended.

Myers-Briggs found that we tend to function at opposite ends of four pairs of preference alternatives:

1. Extravert Versus Introvert

2. Sensing Versus Intuitive

3. Feeling Versus Thinking

4. Perceiving Versus Judging

We have characteristics of all four, but tend to prefer one or the other. These are our personality preferences and determine how we act in different social circumstances and how we interact with others. Below is a brief description of each personality type.

Extravert Versus Introvert

Extraverts - These individuals get a charge from people. They think out loud and are good talkers, but not always good listeners. They process ideas through people and by talking. They need stimulation from interactions with people to keep them motivated and see introverts as cold, uncaring and not friendly.

One of the most rewarding moments for an extravert is to be

around people so he/she can talk and socialize. Because they get a charge from people, they tend to personalize rejection and may have difficulty in sales. However, the paradox is that extraverts are often drawn to sales positions. Because of the high number of rejections in prospecting new business, extraverts can burn out easily before they have truly tested the waters. The challenge for extraverts is to learn not to take rejection personally.

Introverts - These personality types are charged by processing within themselves. They need time alone. They are good listeners and may not speak up with their ideas or thoughts. They tend to see extraverts as time-wasters who state the obvious and talk too much.

Introverts love to work on a computer or go to a movie. They find this much more rewarding then being in a group of people. This can cause problems for them in developing relationships. Their challenge is to develop social skills and work hard to loosen up in social situations and enjoy the company of others.

Sensing Versus Intuitive

Sensing - These people like specific factual answers and information. They are grounded in what is real and actual; they do not relate well to speculation or approximation. They are very literal and do not get caught up in fantasy or what might be. They tend to see intuitive types as daydreamers who are lost and do not have their thoughts in order. This over-reliance on knowledge and facts can limit sensing types as they fail to recognize new options and the creative solutions to problems.

Intuitive - These are creative daydreamers who look at the big picture and tend to jump to conclusions without evaluating all the facts. They rely on intuitive thoughts and feelings to make decisions. Intuitives are visionaries who tend to live in the world of possibilities and what can happen, rather than focusing on what is happening now. They are essential in business and are often leaders or entrepreneurs; however, they must have sensing types around to keep them grounded in reality.

Feeling vs. Thinking

Feeling – They are concerned with others and their emotions. They tend to make decisions based on the feelings of others and themselves. When asked to take action, they will base their decisions on the feelings of other people affected by the decision. They are also concerned with their own feelings and look toward emotional responses to solve problems. Captain Kirk of *Star Trek* is the perfect feeling type as opposed to Mr. Spock, who is the classic thinker.

Thinking – These personality types tend to make decisions based on rational thought and logic. They prefer to solve problems based on logic and reason rather than emotions. They don't understand why people get emotional and may be perceived as cold or uncaring about others. This is probably not the case; they are not likely to base their actions on how others feel about it. Their focus is on logic and results. Does that sound like Mr. Spock?

Perceiving Versus Judging

Perceiving – These people are spontaneous and very adaptive. They love to explore new possibilities and go off the beaten track. They may look disorganized and appear confused, but can actually be very much in control. They start many projects and have difficulty completing them. They have the ability to juggle a lot at one time. At their worst, perceiving types are unorganized, chaotic and unable to complete a task. At their best, they are able to remember many details and accomplish a great many things at one time. They do not understand why judging types have to be so linear in their thinking. It's okay to have a messy desk.

Judging – They are on a schedule and into a routine. They do not like surprises or to go off the beaten path. They know what they plan to accomplish each day and make to-do lists to ensure they get to each task. Judging types will be sure to mark off each item on their list when it is completed and become upset if they do not stay on schedule. They love to complete a job and move on to the next challenge. However, they prefer to focus on the job at hand and not juggle a lot of tasks at one time. Organization is critical to completing a task and an important part of their world. Their desks and offices are in perfect order.

Once again, we all have these characteristics and it is our preference toward one or the other that determines how we act in a given situation. There is no right or wrong and all of these traits can add value. It is important that you understand these personality traits, learn your own preferences and develop a balance in all four areas. This will better help you relate to your customers and prospects and avoid personality barriers with others. Remember it is important to stretch the limits of your comfort zone and learn to express new personality preferences.

This is an area that deserves much more attention. An excellent book for further reading on the subject is *Type Talk at Work* by Otto Kroeger and Janet M. Thuesen.

Action Steps:

1. Read *Type Talk at Work.*

2. Determine your personality profile and how you respond to other's personalities.

3. Expand your comfort zone and learn to tolerate many differ- ent types of personalities.

Chapter 28

Conflict and Customer Service

C onflict is a fact of life. Whether it is in business, sales or personal relationships, disagreements and conflicts are bound to happen. How you respond to these challenges will impact your success in many ways. Your objective should be to diffuse the conflict and provide your customer with a feeling of satisfaction and resolution. The challenge is on the shoulders of the professional sales person to make this happen. Don't expect your customers or prospects to resolve conflict; you must step up and make it happen. Following are a few tips for handling conflict and turning a negative situation into a positive one.

What is Conflict?

This is actually a difficult question to answer because conflict can be very complex. However, it is usually an emotional response based on disagreements between people. We all respond to conflict in various ways, from extreme anger to denial and emotional suppression. The end result is the same; people are left with a negative feeling and a lack of trust. Your goal as a sales professional is to build trust. You can do this if you handle conflict correctly. If not handled properly, trust is lost.

Step One: Listen

The best way to resolve conflict is to begin by listening and attempting to understand the other person's point of view. This may be difficult because many people have a hard time communicating in tense or negative situations. Often times, listening is all you need to do to end the situation and move toward resolution. People tend to diffuse quickly when they feel understood.

Step Two: Do Not Engage

During the disagreement, emotions will flair. It is absolutely critical that you remain calm and professional with an attitude of empathy and understanding. Do not respond to anger with anger. Keep a level head and do not let your emotions get the best of you. This is difficult because your prospect or customer may be expecting you to become angry or emotional and even attempt to get an emotional response from you. Don't go there! Not engaging in the emotional cycle of conflict will often lead to resolution as your customer's emotions de-escalate.

Step Three: Show Understanding

Reiterate to your prospects or customers that you understand and develop empathy for their situations. Tell them that it is your goal to help them solve this problem and that you do not intend to argue or defend your position. Do not assume they know this. Listen with understanding.

Step Four: Clarify

Work to clarify what your prospects are saying. Use phrases like, "If I hear what you are saying..." and "Let me clarify for my sake."

This helps you get a handle on what is happening and better understand. Never make assumptions without clarifying what you think is being said.

Step Five: Focus on the Issue

During a conflict, it is very easy to get lost on tangents such as blame, name-calling and accusations. It is your responsibility to bring the customer back to the real issues at hand. The first four steps are needed before the issue can be dealt with. People cannot rely on logic if there are emotional issues that have not been deflated. When the emotions have settled, move to the actual issues.

Step Six: Find a Solution

At this point, it is time to solve the problem. You will need support from your company and the tools needed to help the customer and resolve the problem. A business puts itself in jeopardy when sales people do not have the resources to solve problems. The final step in conflict resolution is finding a solution and those who deal directly with customers must have the ability to make this happen.

Be prepared to handle conflict. The results can actually be surprising as angry customers make a complete reversal of their positions and become loyal customers. They do this because you gain their trust by handling conflict appropriately and showing them concern and understanding. Conflict is a part of working with people and will arise in sales. All great sales people have had to overcome and deal with conflict in relationships with their prospects, customers, co-workers and others.

Action Steps:

1. Are you ready for conflict? How do you respond when disagreements occur? How do you react to anger from others?
   How do you deal with your own anger?

2. Develop an action plan for dealing with anger and work on
   listening and not engaging with others in conflict. You pull
   your own emotional strings.

3. Practice your conflict plan as much as possible, especially
   when times are most tense.

Chapter 29

Building Trust Results in
Customer Loyalty

Organizations should put their marketing dollars into building trust. Building trust results in customer loyalty, which, in turn, results in more profitable customers and a greater chance for marketing and sales success. Most businesses struggle because trust is not yet present and a loyal customer base has not been developed. This is especially true with start-ups who struggle to build brand awareness, which is a form of trust building. Many of an organization's customers range from merely satisfied to unhappy. Your challenge is to move people into the loyal customer category. This means building trust.

Trust must be present to close the smallest sale, or even to begin a dialogue with a prospect. If nurtured properly, this trust can lead to sales and loyal customers. These customers are loyal because you are meeting their needs and providing them with real benefits.

What is Trust?

Trust is the glue that holds the business relationship together and is expressed repeatedly in your actions. This includes what you do – and do not – do. Simple things are key, such as returning phone calls immediately and being consistent in your words and actions. In this way, trust is an absolutely essential part of sales – and business in general. If trust is not present, customers will not buy. Trust reduces the customer's fear of making the wrong decision. This is a powerful motivating force in prospects and customers.

Trust is an Investment

Building trust is not cheap. It is an investment in your service to customers. This means hiring good people and providing them with ongoing training, offering money back guarantees, and going out of your way to meet customer needs better. The catch is that these investments pay off handsomely in improved profits and a strong referral base. Remember that word-of-mouth marketing is the best way to generate new sales. When trust is high, customers go out of their way to tell others about your business. They become your best referral source.

Learning how to build trust is an investment of time in developing yourself. Reading this book and putting the concepts discussed into action will take effort, but it will be well worth it. This book is a fundamental review of how to build trust, develop relationships with customers and close sales.

Eliminate Customer Sacrifices

What do your customers have to put up with to do business with you? These inconveniences are barriers to success. Look at the companies you are passionate about. How easy is it to conduct business with those organizations? Remove customer sacrifices and build loyal clients. It is very common for companies to place hurdles in front of customers. These hurdles are usually in place not to help the customer, but to save time and money for the organization. Competitive pressures are changing this; however, it is critical for the professional sales person to become a customer advocate and keep things very simple for their customers and prospects.

A good example of this is the banking industry. When I entered the workplace in the early 1980s, banks were open from 9 am to 5 pm. I worked from 8 am to 5 pm. I remember thinking, "How will I ever make it to the bank to deposit my check?" The answer was to leave the office during my work shift. This was a huge inconvenience. Today, my bank is open late in the evening and open on Saturday and Sunday! It is located in my grocery store. This is a trend in business, as the customer takes charge and competition forces the removal of barriers. Remove your barriers to working with customers and prospects and build trust.

Competence and Credibility

Trust is built by showing competence and credibility. Competence is getting the job done right – better than competitors. It is expressed through knowledge of the client's needs, your product/service and the ability to work with others. It is your ability to know your industry and the specifics of the work. Competence is exhibiting proper selling techniques that respect the customer or prospect and work toward adding value and meeting customer needs. Customers feel like you really know what you are doing when you exhibit competence in your work. This builds trust as you are seen as someone who can get the job done right. This does not mean you have to know everything and have all the answers, but it does mean that you should have the resourcefulness to satisfy customer inquiries. More importantly, it means you understand how to get things done for your customer or prospect.

Credibility is your character, integrity and honesty. Only say what you really mean and be a person of integrity. Show genuine concern for the customer through giving and unselfish behavior. The focus is on the customers and their needs. Do not speak badly of others and be held in high regard by all who meet you. These are the components of credibility. This builds trust as customers and prospects turn to people of high character for their business and personal needs. These areas are deeply rooted in who you are, your values and how you trust others.

Customers are Honest When Trust is Present

Don't expect full honesty from people until trust is present. Many objections actually come from a lack of trust. Customers fear that you will take advantage of them if they share their shortcomings or honest concerns with you. When a customer trusts you, he/she is more inclined to tell you how to meet specific needs. If trust is not present, he/she will often withhold information and avoid giving you the real motives behind certain behavior. This is usually the case when you cannot put your finger on why the sale did not close. If trust is not present, there cannot be honest dialogue.

How to Build Trust

Trust is built through frequent interactions. In fact, any interaction you have with customers has an impact on trust. Communication is about trust, not technique. When trust is high, it is effortless; when low, it is a huge burden. As discussed in Chapter 25, listening builds trust because it shows you value the customer. It meets a deep psychological need to be respected as a person. Listening is the single most important thing you can do to build trust. Following are a few more ways to build trust:

- Trust customers to do the right thing.
- Return all phone calls immediately.
- Send thank-you notes.
- Be extremely organized and dependable.
- Do something different and special; be creative.
- Handle complaints promptly with empathy and honesty.

- Offer great customer service.
- Show sincere appreciation.
- Understand your customers.
- Become a valuable resource to the client.
- Create solutions that add value to customers.
- Partner with the customer.
- Create a customer, not a sale.
- Do not over-promise and do what you say you will do.
- Do something that is not expected.
- Always give more than expected.
- Do these things without any expectation of a return from the customer.

Always act in the best interest of your customers. Selling or doing business is the process of building a trusting relationship with people. This is not a passing trend or sales technique, but a way of life.

Action Steps:

1. Make it your challenge to find at least three ways to build trust with customers this week. Write these things down on paper and do them.

2. Develop a "building trust action plan" that outlines specific action steps for building trust in the long term. This includes specific steps you will take with customers to remove hurdles, add value and better meet their needs.

3. Improve your competence, knowledge of your work and credibility, character and ethics. Develop a plan for doing this and put it into action.

Chapter 30

Connect With Customer Vision

This is one of the most important sales and marketing concepts you will read about in this book. This simple, common sense sales tip can turn a business career around. **To increase your sales, get in line with your customer's vision.** If only this powerful concept were easy to put into practice. It is absolutely essential for you to be seen as a resource for your customers and add direct value to them. Let's take a look at how you might find ways to align with your customer's vision and close more sales.

What is Vision?

Vision is how and where we see ourselves in the future. Your prospects and customers have a distinct and powerful vision of their future. Some are very much aware of this vision and can discuss it openly. Others are not so clear. Your job is to uncover and become a part of your customer's vision. You add tremendous value if you help customers discover their vision and make it a reality. As a marketing consultant and sales trainer, I help customers realize their dream of growing their business by increasing sales revenues. A construction contractor might, for example, help your clients realize their dreams of building their new home or office building. An accountant might give you more time to enjoy your family by handling your tax and financial needs. These are examples of how aligning with your customer's vision is an expression of value and direct benefit to customers.

Determine Vision Through Insightful Questions

Ask big picture questions that help you better understand the vision of your customers or prospects. Plan these questions in advance and probe with no assumptions or prejudices that can skew this investigative process. Customers will probably not tell you how to help make their vision a reality. They do not want to appear eager to be sold – or they may not even have a clear vision. They are looking for you to take the initiative and offer the right solution. The customer will see you as a valuable resource when you notice what is important without them having to tell you. This is a real benefit and builds a large amount of trust and confidence. You discover this by asking questions and listening, not by talking. Ask questions about your prospect's or customer's future. "Where do expect to be in the next five years?" "How do you hope to get there?" "How can I be a resource to help you reach your long-term goals?"

How to Discuss Vision on the Sales Call

Additional questions to ask are related to improved profits, return on investment and the customer's vision of the future. Ask straightforward questions about the future of their organization. "What is your vision for the future?" Ask customers to elaborate. Ask about how they can increase profits. "What are the three most important steps you can take to improve your profits?" This will open doors and enable you to be a part of the solution. Ask your customer about his or her comfort zone for buying. This will help you understand how he/she can move from the fear of buying to a desire to purchase. This is a great way to uncover hot buttons.

Help Improve Profits

Showing your business customers how you can improve their profits will go a long way in building trust and creating customer loyalty. The most important business equation is: revenues minus expenses are equal to profits. Work with clients to find ways to improve this equation in their favor. In consumer markets, the equation deals more with desire and fear. People will buy when the desire for owning the product overcomes any apprehension they may have about the purchase. Getting in line with vision will help you uncover solutions that will lead to sales and overcome customer fears. It will lead to an improved quality of life.

Plan, Practice and be Persistent

It is important to prepare a sales strategy that focuses on determining your customer's vision. Write down your questions and script the sales process. Focus on discovering the benefit to the customer. Keep the focus on the customer's perspective and what makes sense to the customer. Get away from your perspective, because it may be wrong. The goal is not to focus on your vision, but rather the vision of the customer.

Use Trial Closes

Help the customer make a decision with trial closes. Ask this great question, "If we are to move forward, how do you see it happening?" Ask "what if" questions and make recommendations based on what the customer has told you. Focus your questions on the client's vision and helping them increase profits or move from the fear of loss to desire for gain. (See Chapter 16 for more information on trial closes.)

Use Caution with Objections and Questions

Be careful with customer objections and questions because they often have a purpose unknown to you. Respond with a question such as, "Is that important to you?" "Why do you ask?" Objections and questions are signals for more information. It is your job to figure out the right answer by probing gently. Resist the need to answer questions immediately because this turns off the buyer. The customer may ask you, "Does it come with leather seats?" You might say, "Yes, yes it does!" The customer may reply, "Well I am looking for cloth." It is better to answer their question with a question, "Are you looking for leather seats?"

Put the Customer in the Driver's Seat

Customers want choices. They want to drive the decision-making process and do not want to be sold, yet they love to buy what is a part of their vision. Aligning yourself with the customer's vision is perhaps the best way to close sales. You become a valuable asset, as you help your customer make their vision of the future a reality.

Action Steps:

1. Prepare a list of probing questions that help you uncover your customer's vision for the future.

2. Find ways to align yourself with their vision and become a valuable resource to help make their vision a reality.

3. Review your vision for the future and how people will help you attain your goals. This concept applies to a customer as well and it is your challenge to determine your role in helping your customer or prospect attain his/her vision. By doing this, your goals will come to fruition. As Zig Ziglar says, "You can get everything in life you want, if you will just help enough other people get what they want."

Chapter 31

Communication in Sales

Proper communication is a complex study worthy of many PhDs. How we communicate is at the center of the sales process. Communication is a two-way street involving a sender and a receiver. To be sure, the best sales people must be excellent receivers, or listeners. They also need to be excellent senders, or presenters, even though they will spend most of their time listening. Becoming an excellent communicator is hard work and should not be taken lightly. Following are a few communication tips that can strengthen your sales skills, helping you to understand customers and eventually close more sales.

It's About Trust

Communication is largely about trust, not technique. When trust is high, it is effortless; when low, it is a huge burden. Have you noticed how communication is easier with people you know and trust? Even if there is a miscommunication, it is resolved easily because of the trust that is central to the relationship. To be a better communicator, find ways to build trust with your customers and nurture relationships. Conversely, to build trust, learn to be a better communicator. It is a circular lock and the key is to become a phenomenal listener. This is especially useful when communicating with people from different cultures or individuals who may not exactly click with you. Take the first step toward understanding where they are coming from, then work to be understood. This is a key principle of building trust and making communication with your customers and prospects an easier process.

Forms of Communication

There are four forms of communication to be aware of and use to connect with customers.

1. Verbal

These are the actual words that are coming out of your mouth. Imagine if the words could be written down on paper and read by your customers, without any non-verbal influence. This is the simplest form of communication and the least important. It is not what you say but how you say it and what they hear that matters. The key areas here are clarity, proper grammar and sentence structure. You do not have to attend Harvard to excel in these areas, but you will need to practice to get it right.

2. Non-Verbal

Most of what is heard during communication is non-verbal, even on the telephone. Non-verbal communication dominates all sales conversations. Studies show only seven percent of communication is expressed via the spoken word; 38 percent is in the tone of voice; and the remaining 55 percent are non-verbal actions. Who you are communicates so loudly that people cannot hear what you are saying. The key is to say what you feel and be honest with what you are trying to accomplish. Your communication should be in line with your intentions.

3. Symbolic

This is the choice of words used to communicate a message. It is a form of non-verbal action and is a powerful way to communicate. Examples include: hot, heat, warm, toasty, burning etc. All of these words are used to describe basically the same thing, but the choice of words makes a difference in how it is understood. All words have symbolic meaning in addition to the actual definition you might find in the dictionary. Be aware of the words you choose and their potential impact on your prospects and customers.

4. Between the Lines

This is the message that needs to be communicated and that must be deciphered to be properly understood. It is what we don't say – or don't know how to say. Professional sales people must be clear and direct. There is no place for game playing in your communications. Prospects and customers may not adhere to this practice; therefore, it is your challenge to learn to intuit or read between the lines. The best way to get to the bottom of the communication is to ask questions and probe. Repeat what you think you heard and let the customer know you are trying to get it right.

Two Major Functions

Communication in sales serves two major functions. One is the actual business at hand – a negotiation or sales transaction. The second, more important function, is how the communication is meeting the emotional needs of your customer or prospect.

1. The Facts

The actual negotiation or sales transaction is the issue on the table and how it is being handled. Most sales people do well in this area, as long as they continue to focus on listening and understanding the other side's point of view. Ask for clarification and make use of intelligent, probing questions. Make sure all the parties agree on the data and terms of the discussion.

2. Emotional Needs

How the communication is meeting the emotional needs of the parties involved in the sale is by far more important because people buy based on emotional needs and benefits. These needs include power, self-esteem, control, fear, and other emotions. The focus needs to be on the buyer and seller to create an efficient, effective outcome. Avoid power struggles and ego-based conflicts and nurture teamwork and shared commitment. This may mean putting your emotional needs aside to better meet the needs of your customer. Remember, we pull our own emotional strings. Nothing can impact a person unless he/she lets it. This is a powerful step to becoming a sales master. It results in communication without judgment or criticism, which draws people to you and makes the communication process easier.

The Customer's Mind

The professional sales person understands that the customer does not share his/her thoughts and feelings about the product or service that is being sold. In order to bridge this gap, you must communicate in the words and thoughts of the customer. Indeed, the sales process evolves out of what is in the customer's mind. Use this to work together toward a mutual agreement.

Become a Spokesperson

Sales people can communicate the message that a product or service effectively meets customer needs and adds value better than any other marketing tool available to organizations. This is done through building relationships with customers and understanding customer needs on a personal level. Proper communication skills are critical to making this happen. Learn the needs of your customers and become an advocate for them in your organization. In this way, you become a spokesperson for the customer and your business.

Dress Down and Dress Up

Your appearance, including your clothing, grooming, jewelry make-up etc. is an expression of who you are and communicates a message to customers. The rule of thumb is to dress in ways that make your customers or prospects feel comfortable. This involves developing an instinct for appropriate dress with various target markets.

I worked with a company who sent sales reps to present to workers in plastics manufacturing facilities. The sales reps wore expensive suits and ties. This was a turn-off to their manufacturing customers who worked mostly in jeans and T-shirts. A more appropriate look for sales reps in this industry would be polo shirts and cotton slacks. Dress in ways that make your customers feel comfortable. On the East coast, jackets and ties still seem to be common. However, a client I worked with in New York City asked me to please dress casually for my visit to his office. There was not a tie to be found in his office, except for one hanging on the door that was worn only with clients who expected to see him wear a tie.

Just Don't Say It

Proper communication is critical to sales success. To become an excellent communicator, it is important to remember that certain phrases and words should be avoided. Most of the time, we use them out of habit – which is okay, because habits can be changed.

Following are a few pointers regarding things not to say and why.

The Put-Down

You are guaranteed to run into interesting people in your sales career. It will be tempting to talk about these people to others and perhaps put them down or poke fun at them. Whatever you say about someone else is a reflection upon you. No matter what happens between you and others, do not put down other people. You can talk about how others are interesting, colorful or on their own path, but a negative statement about them reflects negatively upon you. The psychology behind this is interesting, since we tend to put others down to make ourselves feel good. Find other ways to feel good and find the positive in people.

Always and Never

There really is no "always" or "never" in business. These terms should be avoided, as people see you as rigid and inflexible – or even out of touch with reality. It is rarely appropriate to use these terms and they should be discouraged.

"Please Be Reasonable"

This assumes that someone is not being reasonable. In the person's mind, he/she is being very reasonable. Do not pass judgment on others; rather, work with them toward a solution. Asking people to be reasonable puts them on the defensive and away from agreement. Your challenge is to understand their viewpoint better.

"We All Know" and "The Fact of the Matter"

We don't all know and one should never assume. This statement sounds presumptuous and assumes that your customer or prospect is in the dark. Do not act as if you are better than your customer or prospect and avoid these phrases.

"To Be Honest With You"

There are several variations of this common phrase, such as, "to be frank with you" or "to level with you." This harmless comment leads people to think that maybe you have not been honest in the past. You should always be honest; therefore, there is no need to say that you are going to be honest.

"Yes, but..."

Everything before "but" is negated. Use "and" instead of "but." It sounds better and supports your first comment. This is usually a response to a comment made to you and, as a result, it is very important to support what others say – even if you know it to be incorrect. It is better to acknowledge and validate their thoughts and educate gently. Perceptions are reality.

"Don't Misunderstand Me"

Do not assume that someone does not understand you. The reality is that you have not properly communicated your message. It is your challenge first to understand your customer or prospect and then communicate your message so that it is understood.

"Oh, by the way..."

This is usually a lead-in to something that people do not want to hear. Just come out and say what you need to say and skip this wimpy introduction.

Cussing and Swear Words

There is no place for cussing or swear words in sales or business. It is unprofessional conduct and should not be a part of your vocabulary. Even if it is your customer's habit, do not respond in kind. The negative non-verbal impact will hurt the effectiveness of your communication.

"This is not personal, but..."

Everything is personal in any human interaction. Communication between two people is an intra-personal dialog. Trust is lost when you say it is not personal and then hit the person with the bad news, which almost always follows this comment. Of course it is personal.

As a sales professional, an ongoing study of human communication is an important part of your success. It is just as important to learn what you should not say as it is what you should say. Do this properly and you will rise above the competition.

Action Steps:

1. Be committed to becoming a better communicator and understanding the communication process with your customers and prospects. Take a class, seminar, read a book or listen to audio tapes on communication skills. Your greatest tool in selling is your ability to communicate. Develop these very important skills.

2. Audiotape or videotape yourself communicating with others. Observe how you communicate and learn from this experience. Chances are, you do not come across in the way you think you do.

3. Think before you speak and avoid saying anything negative.

Chapter 32

Competitive Advantage

Customers buy from you because of a distinct advantage you bring to the table over your competition. It is important that you identify this advantage and build on it to advance your business and close more sales. What do you do better than your competitors or peers? What is the unique selling proposition you offer that will bring customers to you? If you can properly identify and develop your competitive advantage, you are almost assured sales and marketing success. Let's take a closer look at the fundamentals of competitive advantage.

Value to Clients

Your competitive advantage should link directly to how you add value to your clients. The specific benefits that your clients are pursuing should be found in your competitive advantage. Indeed, this will help customers differentiate you from competitors and give them a reason to do business with you. It also builds trust as they realize that you understand their needs. For example, you may be selling pizza to customers in your area. The combination of price, service and product quality will establish your competitive advantage. If you cannot do any of these three things better than your competition, then your business selling pizza will suffer. Imagine you found that there is a high demand for pineapple pizza that was not being met by your competitors. Offering pineapple would become your competitive advantage – at least in the short term. Seek ways to improve your service or product and better meet your customers' needs.

Marketing Plan

A competitive advantage is an important part of your marketing plan and sales strategy. It is the core piece of value that you bring to customers and your principal selling proposition. Your marketing plan should include a clearly written competitive advantage. This message should also be communicated in your sales presentations, marketing promotions and on your Web site. You might even make it a part of your mission statement. Inform people about the uniqueness of your business and how you can meet their needs better then others with similar products or services.

Competitive Analysis

An important step is a complete analysis of the competition. Who is the competition? How can the company gain a competitive edge? Has the competition been researched? What are the results of research on the competition? Look at your competitors and your common target market. How can you provide something to this target market that your competitors missed or cannot provide? Gather this competitive intelligence and make the changes needed to meet client needs better. Those changes may include pricing, market position, distribution, product or promotional modifications, to name a few.

Listen to customers and develop them into a source of competitive intelligence. Customers will generally tell what they like and do not like about your competition. These comments are incredibly valuable clues that help you develop a competitive advantage. It is perfectly legal and ethical to gather competitive data. Most of this information can be gathered directly from the Internet and your competitor's Web sites. In fact, according to *Sales and Marketing Management* magazine, the No. 1 use of the Web by business managers is competitive intelligence. In developing your Web site, review your competitor's sites and find ways to improve your site from a customer perspective. (See Section IV for more detailed information regarding the Web and how to use it as a sales tool.)

New Markets

The development of a competitive advantage and your competitor research may very well lead to the discovery of new markets for your products and services. This may be critical to augment your business. It will also give you a better understanding of how you compete in your current markets. Don't be afraid to transition your target market as needed to develop a strong competitive advantage. Remember, one of the basic laws of marketing is that you cannot be all things to all people. You will get the best sales results by focusing on a specific target market where you have a significant competitive advantage.

The Ultimate Competitive Advantage

Relationships built on trust are probably the most powerful competitive advantages you can develop with customers. **Even if your product or service is indistinguishable from your competition, your relationship with customers can set you apart.** This is becoming more important in today's competitive environment, as prices equalize among competitors and products become more alike. In service-based industries, the relationship and quality of work are keys to developing a winning competitive advantage.

Action Steps:

1. Research your competition and make a competitive grid that ranks your business with your direct competitors, based on how well you meet the specific needs of your target market and add value to customers. From this research, clearly outline your competitive advantage and better identify your target market.

2. Communicate your competitive advantage to your customers and prospects. Put energy, time and money into clearly understanding and communicating your competitive advantage. It will help you rise to the top in your market because you are communicating to customers what they need to hear before they will do business with you.

3. Develop yourself and learn to build effective relationships with others; this could be your greatest competitive advantage.

Part IV:

Selling and
the Internet

Chapter 33

Web Site Marketing: Create a Web Site That Gets Results

The next few chapters will review how you can benefit from the Internet and an effective Web site. These new technologies are powerful complements to your selling and marketing skills because they are of tremendous value to your customers and prospects. It is also a great asset to you as a cost-effective marketing tool that provides unlimited reach, new channels of interactive communication and much more. The bottom line is this: if used properly, the Internet can help you reach new customers and close more sales.

We are in the middle of a sales and marketing revolution, and it is still in the early stages. The Internet has quickly become a powerful sales channel and support to personal selling efforts. However, the majority of businesses and sales people still have not tapped into this opportunity. Even with the tremendous potential of the Internet, most companies are falling short of their Web site sales potential. Many business owners fear the new technology or do not access the Internet. It is invisible to many; yet millions of others are buying and selling via the Internet.

The Internet has seen tremendous growth for a sales medium that only hit mainstream a few years ago. Pick up a current copy of the *Wall Street Journal* or go on-line to www.internet.com to see the current data. Just about anything that can be sold is over the Internet. Forty to 50 percent of households are currently on-line and that number is expected to grow to 70 percent by 2003. These are afflu-ent households looking for value through the Internet. They want to save time, are looking for convenience, and are comfortable with mini-mal risk. This represents phenomenal business and selling opportuni-ties. These trends are also true in business communities, as more com-panies move on-line. Whether sales come directly or indirectly from your Web site, the Internet is the critical marketing and sales medium of the future. It is the first choice of young people today when searching for information and making buying decisions. The Web will not replace the selling principles discussed here; however, it will complement your selling strategies and it is one of your greatest tools for distributing information to customers and prospects. Following are a few tips for creating a Web site that generates sales.

Develop a Web Site Strategy

Create specific goals for your site and develop an Internet mar-keting and sales plan. What do you want your site to do for your business? How can sales be generated from the site? Many compa-nies only exist on the Web; others have very passive sites that func-tion as company brochures on-line. Develop a strategy that goes beyond providing company information and stimulates sales for your business. Web sites can be simple brochure-ware, content-rich information centers or complete, interactive sales mediums. Any of these three strategies can lead to sales success. Choose the strategy that best fits your marketing model.

Meet Customer Needs

Put yourself in the shoes of your customers. What do your cus-tomers want to see in your site? Ask your customers this question via a suggestion form on your site. The Internet is the most powerful communication medium on the planet. Fill your site with information that pushes customers' hot buttons and adds value to their busy lives. My site (www.SalesTrainingPlus.com) contains dozens of pages of useful sales and marketing information that visitors can use today in their work. This adds value to my clients and brings people back to the site for the latest updates. What information are your customers looking for? If you are in residential real estate, then your customers probably want to learn as much as possible about homes for sale in their area. Stay in tune with the specific information that is being searched and researched by your target market and provide that information on your Web site. This builds tremendous trust and can help your customers and prospects.

How to Get Hits

Maintain good meta tags and register with key search engines at least once every two months. Look into Web Position Gold™, a search engine submission software program that will help bring visitors to your site. Ask your Web master to research this program and submit your site on a regular basis. Promote your site in all your advertising and promotions and ask people to visit the site. Make your Web site a part of your sales process and discussions with customers and prospects. People enjoy looking up sites and surfing the Web and most of your serious prospects will be happy to review your Web site for information. Research Internet malls, portals and directories. Email articles to other relevant "ezines" (electronic newsletters) and include a reference and link to your site within the articles. Advertise your site through reputable people who have established emailing lists on the Web. If your site is good, word-of-mouth will bring interested visitors. Track the activity on your site with traffic reports that should be provided by your Web master or hosting company. Companies such as Super Stats (www.SuperStats.com) provide excellent traffic reports and analysis.

Make Your Site Interactive

Include your email address and phone number on all pages on the site. It should be very easy for customers to contact you via the Web site. Allow visitors to submit information to you via a form or questionnaire that helps assess their needs. If you have products to sell, establish a secure server and take credit cards for payment. Respond promptly to all inquiries, either by email or via the phone. If you cannot respond in less than a day, your competitors probably will. If possible, sell your products directly on-line with an on-line shopping cart or order form.

Review Your Competitor's Sites of Internet Users

The Internet easily allows you to research, find and evaluate your on-line competitors. Develop a competitive advantage by reviewing your competitors' sites and creating your own that better meets customer needs. Customer choices run the Web and sites that better meet customer needs will be successful. The Internet revolution is customer-driven. It is the essence of a free market system with little government involvement. This is a great opportunity for you and your company to begin reaching customers 24 hours a day, seven days a week – and to do it better than your competitors.

Keep it Simple

Your site should be easy to navigate and make good use of white space. Do not use fancy graphics or photos that take more than 20-30 seconds to download, unless they are compelling. Currently, less than five percent of Internet users have high-speed access. Quick download of the site is absolutely essential. Fight the urge to get carried away with sizzle on your site. Focus on the goals of the site, meeting customer needs and adding value. Content is more important than flash.

The Internet holds incredible business opportunities for those who want to reach customers and turn great ideas into millions of dollars. It is changing the way we do business. The remaining chapters in this section will help with more details needed to establish an Internet sales and marketing plan. Catch the Internet wave and find new channels of sales success.

Action Steps:

1. Get customer feedback on your Web site. Does it meet their needs? Is it easy to understand and navigate? How can it be improved? What content would customers like to see on the site?

2. Design a customer feedback submission form for your site to collect data from visitors.

3. If you do not have a Web site, find a way to integrate a customer friendly site into your sales efforts.

Chapter 34

Bring Visitors to Your Web Site

Now that you have developed a great looking Web site that meets the needs of your customers, its time to get the word out and bring visitors to your site. It's great to have a Web site loaded with benefits for potential customers, but if there are no visitors, then no one benefits. This includes the sales team, the site's owner and developer!

There are two key methods for generating visitors to your site. One involves search engine registration and visibility. The other involves your proactive marketing of your site. Let's take a closer look at how to bring visitors to your site.

Search Engines: Do the Right Thing

Registering with the major search engines is obviously very important. However, that alone will not secure hits or visitors. Your site should be search engine friendly. It is important to research the key words and phrases people are using to find sites like yours. Your site should be content-rich with those same key words and phrases. Work with your Web site developer to set up a specific search engine strategy. This should be included in the design of your site and in monthly registrations to all the major search engines. You should receive a monthly report of your site's placement in the key search engines under various search terms. Do not leave your search engine strategy to chance. Top Web sites get good exposure because of a strong search engine strategy.

Word-of-Mouth is Powerful

Sales and marketing professionals know that word-of-mouth referrals are the most powerful forms of personal marketing. Good Web sites are promoted by word-of-mouth. Encourage people to visit your site and tell others about it. If you are selling products on your site, offer discounts for referred business and other incentives to draw in visitors. Remind visitors to bookmark the site and return for updates and new information. Update your visitors with dates and times of upcoming events, features, articles and other areas of interest. They will recommend others to your site for value-added content.

Write Articles

Find publications that are being read by your target market and submit articles. Include in your article a byline with your site address listed as a resource for more information. These articles can be written in traditional newsletters, magazines, newspapers and also ezines, which are electronic magazines on the Internet. Editors are always looking for interesting and informative content. Keep your articles to about 400-600 words; be specific to your topic with a sincere desire to help, teach and inform. If you or your company does not have interesting things to write about, why should anyone visit your Web site?

Include Articles on Your Site

Interesting articles provide value to readers and help search engines find your site by adding more key words. These articles should inform readers about important issues in their area of expertise. Whether or not your articles are published, post new articles on your site once or twice a month. Also, submit these articles to portals and resource sites that are visited by your target market. As the Internet grows and additional Web sites are added to the net, content will be in high demand. Take advantage of this trend and place value-added articles in front of your target markets on the Web.

Web Site Advertising

Advertise for your site in very targeted, traditional and on-line media. Use call-to-action ads that encourage the prospective customer to visit your site. Do not attempt to sell your product or services in these ads; rather, use the ads to bring people to the Web site. Let the Web site do the selling. The sales team can then develop the relationship and follow-up to close the sale.

Develop Alliances

Link exchanges and portals are a good way to get exposure for your site. Create links to your site and develop alliances, or partnerships, with other sites. Be careful with your links, as visitors may leave your site and not return. Look for high-traffic sites that can increase your visibility with a link to your site. There may be a fee associated with this; however, the rewards could be well worth your investment.

Keep it Fresh

New content and site redesign are the oxygen of the Internet. Pay someone to do it if you don't have the time. A forgotten Web site is a waste of money and will not show returns. Update information on your site often because visitors are turned off by stale sites.

Monitor Your Site's Visitors

Be ready to invest time and money in the promotion of your site. Often, this can be your best advertising expense, as targeted customers visit your informational and benefit-loaded Web site. These visitors can become loyal customers, providing sales leads, prospects and long-term business for your company.

Action Steps:

1. Develop a marketing plan to promote your Web site. Develop a search engine placement strategy and a tradi-tional advertising program.

2. Research the key words being used by your target market to find your site. Fill your site with these key words and submit them to the search engines using Web Position Gold™ or a similar software program.

3. Research and collect a list of publications that are read by your target market and develop an ad for these and other media sources that pull people into your site.

4. Contract the services of a respected Internet marketing com-pany to help promote your site.

5. Visit www.goto.com and learn about pay–for–position search engine strategies. This is a very powerful method for driving traffic to your Web site in a cost–effective manner.

Chapter 35

Make Your Web Site a Sales Tool

The recent turbulence in the stock market has left many people questioning the real impact of the Internet on business. Well-designed Web sites with many visitors are not usually enough to support an entire business model or generate profits. Internet stock prices, especially for e-retailers, have dropped dramatically in recent months – and this is a good thing. Many of these overvalued e-companies were not following sound marketing and sales strategies. The businesses that survived the initial Internet craze are those that know how to implement marketing strategies that work on and off the Internet. Following are a few key suggestions for developing an Internet marketing strategy that leads to sales.

Develop an Internet Marketing Plan

The first step is to develop a clear understanding of what you want your Web site to do for your business and your sales. There is no magic bullet or quick-fix. Integrating a Web site into your sales and marketing strategy takes work. The first step is to determine the specific benefits to your target market, or visitors, to your Web site. Do you want your site to be an on-line brochure, information resource or interactive tool? Answer these questions from the perspective of your customers.

The Web Site Supports Your Sales Channels

It is absolutely critical that your Web site supports your sales channels, such as your sales team, direct mail, re-sellers, telemarketing and other channels. Many companies have Web sites that actually compete with existing channels. This is a lose-lose scenario and leads to sluggish sales and confused customers. Retailers, or re-sellers, are often hurt the most. Your Web site should function as a powerful complement and support to your sales efforts.

Qualify Buyers on the Web

Prospective customers who have reviewed your site are more likely to buy. In this way, the site functions as a qualifier and needs analysis tool. Potential customers have their questions answered and should be ready to make a buying decision. One of the best-qualified visitors to your site is a prospect who has been directed to the site by a sales rep. This visitor will have a specific reason for coming to the site and is usually converted into a sale.

Sales Objections are Handled On-Line

When objections arise, the sales rep can send people to the Web site. A good site will build credibility and allow the customer to look at the information with no pressure to respond or act at that time. A Web site that pushes customer hot buttons will help ease objections and build trust and confidence that you can help. Email is another great way to handle objections. It lets the customer stay in control and relaxes the pressure. Customers and prospects can review your Web site and email on their schedule. Always validate the objection in your message. These two methods are also a great way to qualify potential clients and handle objections; if they do not take the time to read your email or visit your Web site, then they probably are not going to move forward with your sales proposition.

Quality is Better than Quantity

On the Web, it is much better to work with a few quality customers than to be inundated with inquiries and visitors who have no intention of doing business with you. It is important to set up a quality promotion strategy for the site, including a search engine strategy that will bring quality visitors. Do not just go for massive hits, or you will be bogged down and waste valuable time responding to useless inquiries. Focus on quality over quantity and tapping into your target market.

These are just a few tips regarding developing a successful Internet sales and marketing plan. Despite the fluctuations on Wall Street, the Internet is still the most powerful marketing tool of the new century and companies that get it right will thrive.

Action Step:

1. **Establish a focused Web site marketing strategy that gets results and is targeted to meet the needs of your customers and prospects.**

Chapter 36

How to Close Sales With Your Web Site

As mentioned earlier, the Internet is currently the most dominant force in marketing. Yet, most companies are struggling to implement the strategies needed to make their Web sites pay off and increase their business. We know that the first step is to bring visitors to your site. The best method to increase a site's visibility is through old-fashioned sales and marketing; there is no quick fix. The sales professional makes use of the Web site to increase sales and attract new customers. He/she does this by using their site as a closing tool. Following are a few tips regarding how to use the Internet and your Web site to close sales.

Design a Web Site that Pushes Customer Hot Buttons

The Web site should meet customer needs and build excitement about your products or services. This is absolutely critical, because the sales process may stall when a potential customer visits a poorly designed site. Develop a site that gets rave reviews and works for customers. Get outside of your box and get feedback from folks other than your site developer, friends or co-workers. Get feedback from customers. They will decide if your site adds value with a click of their mouse. The site cannot help you close sales unless it pushes customer hot buttons. These hot buttons should result in a call to your sales team or a direct sale. Keep the site simple, easy-to-use and straightforward. Do not over think your Web site; it must be easy to use and save time, not create headaches.

Send Everyone to Your Site

Be proud of your site when talking to customers and prospects. This confidence is expressed in how you ask people to visit the site. If you believe in your site's ability to push hot buttons, your customers will believe. Send anyone you meet to your site. If the site pushes hot buttons, then the sales process will be much easier. Make sure there is something of value on the site for each visitor. This will usually come in the form of expert advice or knowledge about your product or service, not just self-promoting content.

Deflect Sales Objections with Your Web Site

When objections arise, send people to your Web site for answers. Always validate the objection and let the customer know where to go on the site for help. Inform them that others have had the same concerns and the Web site will clarify the situation. This educates the customer about how your company can help them. The Web site will allow the customer to look at the information with no pressure to respond or act. It lets the customer stay in control. A good Web site that pushes customer hot buttons will help ease objections and build the customer's confidence.

Use the Site to Build Trust

The site should support your sales process by building trust. This trust is built through credibility and competence, which is the key to building trust and reducing objections. A well-designed site communicates to your customers that you know what you are doing and you understand their needs. This builds competence by expressing to your customer that you know how to help them. It also builds credibility by showing that you have the savvy and knowledge to build a Web site that works. Customers will return to your site because it provides valuable knowledge.

Web Sites Qualify Prospects

The Internet is still very young and there is some novelty to having a Web site, as not everyone has one – yet. Prospects that are interested in doing business with you will visit your site. This is a great way to qualify potential clients. If they do not take the time to visit your Web site, then they probably are not going to buy or move forward with the project. Customer feedback about your site will be very helpful as you assess their needs. However, don't give up on prospects who do not visit your site; rather, learn from this process.

Follow Up With Email

Use benefit-oriented emails to connect with customers. Email is non-threatening and very customer-focused because the clients can respond on their time. Be direct with email and focus on benefits to the customer. Write about how you can help. Use the customer's name and avoid referring to yourself too often in your email message. The email should clearly express what you are going to do for your customers and how it will be a direct benefit to them.

This is an exciting time for sales and marketing professionals. Research and develop effective Internet marketing strategies and watch your sales grow.

Action Steps:

1. Develop a Web site you can be proud of and that will build trust with customers. This will lead to more inquiries and more sales. Develop your site from your customer's perspective and not your own. Many Web sites are difficult to use, hard to understand and navigate simply because they were not created from the customer's perspective.

2. Set-up a focus group of your best customers and new prospects and ask them to critique your site and provide you with ideas for making the site a better marketing tool.

3. Read books, attend seminars and train yourself to become an expert in Internet marketing. As we look to the future, it is the most important part of sales and marketing.

Chapter 37

Sales Tips for Technical Professionals

The growth of technology's importance in our economy has led to a surge of high-tech jobs and new technology companies. Just like any other business, these companies must learn to market and sell their products to survive. This chapter reviews a few basic concepts that are critical to understand for those selling in high-tech markets – especially those people who are transitioning into sales from a high-tech position.

Competitive Pressures Force High-Tech Professionals into Sales

In today's competitive, high-tech markets, it is very common for technical professionals to find themselves in a selling role. If you are a high-tech professional, it may not be enough to be skilled in technical areas. You may be required to become involved in marketing and sales arenas. If this is the case, it becomes essential to develop proficient selling and relationship skills. This may come as a surprise, but high-tech pros are actually well-suited for sales. The challenge is learning how to sell and believing you can do it. Following are a few tips that can help your transition into a sales and marketing role in your company.

Learn the Basics of Professional Selling

Learning how to sell and developing customer relationship skills can be intimidating to high-tech professionals. Many have never dealt with customers in a sales or marketing capacity. They fear the unknown and dislike the thought of having to become a "pushy" sales person selling to vulnerable prospects. Understanding the power of professional selling can elevate this fear. Begin by learning the nuts and bolts of selling. You will be surprised to learn that selling is very much an analytical process – much like high-tech endeavors.

Belief in the Product's Benefits is a Given

One of the most fundamental parts of sales is a strong belief in your product or service. A thorough understanding of high-tech processes results in extensive product knowledge. This is critical, because it is necessary first to understand a product or service before you can believe in it 100 percent. The technical professional's high product knowledge provides a very important asset in selling effectively. Selling the benefits of a complex product is key to success in high-tech sales.

Selling is Art and Science

The sales process can be very enlightening for high-tech professionals who are making the transformation from things to people. This is true because selling is actually a very analytical process. Analytical skills can be a great asset and many high-tech professionals will come to realize they have many natural and necessary selling skills. First, they need to learn the sales process properly. Selling involves prospecting, tracking your contacts, presenting effectively, handling objections and closing. Basically, these are all the areas outlined in this book. These processes are actually very logical in nature. It is important to evaluate what works and what doesn't. The key is to learn the sales process and develop a strategic selling plan that can be implemented into day-to-day selling activities. This is the easy part.

How to Develop Relationship Skills

The difficult part is the creative or artistic side of selling, which involves developing a relationship with customers (review Part III). Creativity is essential as you learn to problem solve, build trust and meet the needs of your customers. This, too, can be learned and the proper skills can be developed. The bottom line is you must develop yourself before you can develop effective relationships. This includes learning how to get inside the head of your customer. Ask questions, listen, provide solutions, understand their real problems and work with them to uncover solutions and better meet their needs. This is not magic. It is the simple task of serving customers – the secret to building relationships and trust. Many analytical people are focused on what is happening in their own heads. To be successful in sales, you must get out of your head and into the heads of your prospects and customers. This transition will not be easy; however, the analytical skills of the high-tech professional can help you to become a sales master.

Probe, Listen and Build Trust

The most important of these analytical skills will be the ability to probe and explore your customer's hot buttons. You should follow up by taking notes and listening very attentively. This will build trust and make the close easier. See this as an analytical process of uncovering needs to help customers and prospects better. **This book reviews many of these processes; now you must put them into action.**

A High-Tech Sales Career Brings High Rewards

The rewards of selling high-tech products and services can be tremendous. Popular, high price-point items can lead to healthy commission pay-outs, repeat customers and a rewarding work experience as you help your customers do their jobs better. Embrace a commission-based compensation system. Although a base salary provides short-term security, it cannot provide unlimited earning potential. What job is secure in today's turbulent market? Effective sales and marketing skills will always bring high rewards in high-tech markets. In fact, professionals who possess both analytical and relationship skills are in extremely high demand. Develop your selling skills as a high-tech professional and reach new levels of success.

Action Steps:

1. **Become a student of selling. Attend training courses, read more books and magazines and listen to tapes. Become committed to learning to sell. Successful sales people are trained and developed, not born.**

2. **Focus on learning how to build trust and develop effective relationships through listening and using your analytical skills for problem solving.**

3. **You must make the realization that success for your high-tech business will only come through effective sales processes, which will often involve personal selling skills.**

Part V:

Conclusion

Chapter 38

Future Sales Trends

U ndeniably, how products and services are sold in the future will change. We cannot predict how it will manifest itself, but we do know change is coming – usually before we are prepared. However, there is a solution: planning in the present helps us to prepare for the future. Plan ahead for trends and be better prepared for the future. Following are a few selling trends that will play a major role in your sales success today and in the future.

Say Hello to the Real Boss: The Customer

Customers will drive business outcomes in the future – even more than they do today. An incredible number of buying options put real power in the hands of the customer. If organizations cannot meet customer needs or add value, the customer can easily move on. The roles and responsibilities of sales people will expand and grow in importance as they become the voice of the customer. Customer needs and the marketplace itself will drive high-tech innovations, not venture capitalists or savvy marketing companies. These high-tech solutions, both hardware and software, must have practical, common sense applications if they are to succeed in the market place.

Sales techniques and marketing quick fixes are out. Soft sell, partnerships and relationship building with customers are the coming trends. The goal is to partner with the customer. Partnerships are built on trust, immediate problem solving, frequent contact, honest communications, and a win-win relationship. Relationships of this nature meet needs and add value to the customer. No longer can customers be thought of as a tool for personal gain. Rather, the focus must be on the customers' gain and making the customers' needs the key issue.

It is the customer who pays your salary and determines your company's future. The best way to meet customer needs is to ask the customer, "How can our company add value or better meet your needs?" Then do it better than your competitors.

Those Who Adapt and Change will Lead the Pack

Sales people must change to improve. This is done through continuous learning and development. Those who do not change or adapt will struggle and stagnate as others pass them by. Self-development and personal evolution will be pronounced among the sales leaders. This will enable you to adapt to complexity and stay ahead of change by observing and predicting trends before they occur. Change is the only constant in business. Sales people who properly adapt to change will thrive. The best method for success during turbulent times is personal learning, growth and development.

Prepare for the Internet

The Internet has become the most powerful marketing tool in history. It could be the most powerful development since the assembly line, the automobile or the telephone. Electronic commerce and marketing over the Internet are still in their infancy. This is an excellent opportunity to expand your marketing reach. There will be tremendous growth as a generation that grew up with computers begins to enter the marketplace. Instant communications, speed, increased information and incredible accessibility make the Internet and email a must in today's business environment. The future will be a time of immediate and personalized satisfaction. Customers want it now and technology will satisfy that gratification. Smart sales people know this and are high-tech savvy and on-board with new technologies.

Creativity will be Rewarded

Creativity is the spark that will augment your sales. Sales people who are proactive innovators and create new value will thrive. Only 10 percent of sales people are true innovators who are proactive in their markets and action-oriented. We all have innate creative abilities. Tap that creativity and develop strategies that will result in business success and prosperity. These leaders will create change and force competitors to adapt or fall behind.

Prosperity Comes to Those Who Are Having Fun

Successful sales people realize that they are motivated because they enjoy what they are doing. These folks do not work just for the money, security or ego boost. They work because it is fun. This will become the culture of successful sales teams in the future. Find ways to make selling productive and fun. This happens when you are doing what you love.

Values and Ethics

Customers will increasingly demand trust, honesty and ethical responsibility from sales people. Those who do not comply will be hurt in the marketplace. Lying, unethical tactics and lack of integrity will be observed by smart and intuitive customers. Customers will demand honesty and true benefit. Evaluate your principles, values and virtues.

Other Trends:

- Increased cost of direct mail will result in more targeted marketing and less "junk" mail.

- Telemarketing will increase because it is cost-effective and because it can be easily be measured.

- Labor shortages will continue and more people will work from their homes.

- Price is more important and more closely tied to customers' perceived value.

- Supply will continue to exceed demand and keep prices and inflation low.

- Global selling will continue to rise.

Sales professionals must learn from the past, live in the present and plan for the future. Applying intelligent focus in these areas can help you prepare for the future by living in the future today.

Action Steps:

1. Where will you be in the next three months, in the next year, two years and five years? Be prepared to answer this question or miss your opportunities.

2. Are you prospering from the Internet? Find ways to make the Web a part of your business.

3. Begin preparing for your future today by putting in place a plan that will allow you to bring more value to your customers and prospects in the future.

Chapter 39

Personal Action Plan

The concepts and ideas discussed in this book must be put into action for you to reach higher levels of sales success. It is my hope that you will take these concepts and build them into a personal action plan. Otherwise, you may have wasted your time reading this book! Refer to the "Sales Action Plan" worksheet at the end of this chapter and the individual action plans throughout the book to help you set goals, strategies and identify the steps needed to put your plan into action. Following are a few tips regarding making this plan reality and living your dreams.

Time and Nature

A personal action plan sets the foundation for you to accomplish anything you want in life, given two fundamental limitations: time and the laws of nature. It will take time to convert your thoughts and goals into reality. We also must realize that there are certain fundamental laws of nature and genetics that we cannot change. Otherwise, the sky's the limit. Setbacks will happen along the way; however, remember you control your responses to life. Success is not easy and anyone who can claim it has worked hard and suffered many setbacks. It is often how we overcome those challenges that determines success. This is expressed in your attitude. Nothing is easy and all good things take hard work and effort. However, this action plan should be work you love. Your mission, goals and action plan should be fun and fulfilling. It stops being work. Selling should be fun because it is in tune with your mission and you help others. If this is not true for you, then find something that is fun.

Set a Direction

The first step is to identify clearly what you want to accomplish. This is your goal or mission. It can be anything you wish, but it must be concrete and measurable. You can set several of these goals for yourself as a sales professional or in other parts of your career. An example might be to increase your annual income by 30 percent. This is a very tangible goal. It can be measured, and there are probably no limits placed on you doing this – other than the limits you impose upon yourself. The key factor in making this happen will be your strategy.

Establish a Winning Strategy

Your strategy determines if you will be effective and successful in accomplishing your goal. It is the "how" that describes the focus of making your goals a reality. The genius is almost always found in the approach to the situation or strategy. If you want to increase your income by 30 percent, you have many choices to select from to make this happen. Your strategy revolves around how you choose to make your goal a reality. It is very reasonable to increase your sales production by 30 percent by becoming better trained in selling and/or your product and services. This, then, is your strategy. The next step is to list the very specific action steps of your strategy.

Specific Steps

The actual steps needed to reach your goals should be well-defined within your plan. These are the specific things you will need to accomplish to implement your strategy. This could mean attending meetings, engaging in phone calls and maintaining a detailed to-do list. Each specific goal has an action plan. If you were to become better trained, you might attend a seminar, work with a top producer, read books, listen to tapes or go back to school. These things will not happen unless you plan them. Set a timeframe to keep you on track and build accountability. Set goals for both short-term and long-term projects.

Don't Go it Alone

No one is ever highly successful without relying on the help of others. As you go about establishing these action steps, realize that you can get help and recruit people to help you accomplish tasks. Find ways to delegate to others and build a support team that helps implement your strategy. Find a person who has reached the level of success you are pursuing and ask what he/she does. Include these things in your action plan. Be around successful people and copy what they do. Add your own personal touch and find ways to improve what they do.

Measure Your Results

Set measurement systems. This helps you know if you are on track. This is a critical area because many people tend to limit themselves by setting standards that are too low. Work this through with others and set challenging, realistic measurement standards. Increasing your income by 30 percent can be broken down into a number that can be measured daily, weekly and monthly.

Sales Action Plan

Goal: (What I want to accomplish)

Strategy: (How am I going to do it?)

Action Plan: (Steps needed to make it happen)

Action Step	Date Due

Measurements System: (How will I know when I am there?

Action Steps:

Follow the guidelines in the chapter and complete the "Sales Action Plan" worksheet and begin moving toward making your dreams come true.

1. **Write a goal.**

2. **Develop a strategy.**

3. **Set specific Action Plan steps.**

4. **Develop a time-line.**

5. **Establish a measurement system.**

6. **Make it happen.**

Chapter 40

Wood-Young Consulting Sales Training Programs and Consulting Services

This chapter will review the sales training programs provided by Wood-Young Consulting. These programs help you put into action the selling concepts discussed in this book. On-site workshops are held at your organization's location and public workshops bring the training to a mix of marketing and sales professionals.

Mission, Values and Core Beliefs

When hiring an outside consultant, or sales trainer, it is very important to understand their values and core beliefs. Following are the key principles, values and guidelines of the Wood-Young Consulting team.

The core business values are built on honesty, integrity, trust, persistence and hard working implementation that leads to results. Action-orientation and a focus on the big-picture analysis are highly valued. The idea of an outside, creative approach to an organization's business is appreciated. The importance of listening, asking questions and clarifying is a key value. Also, communicating with empathy, understanding and a focus on the clients and their needs are critical. Helping clients and building solid relationships are highly important attributes.

Wood-Young Consulting Mission Statement:

"Increase client revenues by providing sales and marketing training and consulting services."

Part of the mission is to contribute to the personal and professional development of sales and marketing professionals and teams through the use of facilitated, customized learning sessions, meetings and written materials. The other part is to utilize talents, experience, abilities and knowledge to add value to organizations through marketing, sales and management consulting, project management, and training services. Results are measured in changed behavior and improved sales.

Sales Training Program Mission Statement:

The mission of the sales training program is to add value to sales professionals by facilitating training that enables them to improve themselves and their job performance. Programs are tailored to the specific needs of the sales person, team, organization and marketplace. The program takes a comprehensive view of the sales environment and is not a quick fix, but a results-based approach that incorporates the best in professional development and sales training. We hope to enhance the lives of sales and marketing professionals.

The Choice of Professional Development

Professional development is absolutely critical in business – especially in sales. Sales people are rewarded in direct proportion to their service to clients. The best way to increase their value is to develop their abilities and skills. This leads to increased rewards. Today's competitive business environment forces sales organizations to improve constantly – or fail. The training programs meet those needs by providing a comprehensive, effective sales training and motivational program that will stimulate this learning process and continued self-development. This is important because individuals learn when they want to learn. The training program must stimulate the awareness of this need to learn and change.

The training can change a person's life. It is designed to build a new foundation in one's professional life and in the appropriate direction. We all have the power to make decisions. This is the starting point of the training program. Individuals learn how to invest their time in the right balance. Success in sales is not handed out on a silver platter; rather, learning and contributing are the paths to the attainment of goals. This program teaches sales people to follow their conscience. They learn how to follow their mind, body, heart and soul. This will give them the direction and wisdom to accomplish great things. This is intuitive selling at its best.

Selling is a Skill to be Learned

In the right environment, strong training sessions, workshops and seminars motivate sales people. However, effective selling and sales management cannot be taught quickly. We are not born to be effective sales people; these traits must be learned. There are no quick fixes, easy tricks or luck over the long term. They must be learned through experience and the growth of natural talent. Selling effectively means doing the right thing at the right time. There is no one method that will work all the time; the approach needs to change and adapt to the situation. The best approach to selling is a well-balanced, big-picture view of the situation and circumstances. A holistic approach to sales and sales training is critical. However, there are wrong and right ways of doing things; this is also true in sales. Sales approaches can range from terrible to excellent.

The Art and Science of Sales

Selling is both science and art. It is an analytical and a creative process. Selling is science because there are proven approaches that work. Deduction, observation and analytical skills are very important to selling, as they are in science. In many ways, selling is a numbers game; it is an exercise in presenting to enough prospects until someone buys. Yet, it is also an art, because creativity and spontaneity are keys to success in sales. The marketplace, business in general, and sales are constantly changing and creativity is needed to adapt to these changes. The sales rep who is centered, balanced and maintains an inner sense of purpose, focus and peace will best adapt in today's chaotic business environment. Dealing with people is a skill of communication and a balance of dealing with emotions, uncertainty and individual uniqueness. Individuals who are creative and think beyond the boundaries (outside of the box) will discover new ways to succeed. These new initiatives will lead to growth, well beyond expectations.

Selling is Service

Selling is based on helping customers and adding value to their already busy and complex lives. Selling tactics of the past are outdated and ineffective. The sales training program takes into account the current trends in business and presents a new model for selling. Sales professionals need to make trust and excellent service part of who they are and how they conduct business. When this is accomplished, the return will be greater than the investment. The paradox of sales is this: give and it will be returned to you many times over. Sales people benefit from helping and giving to others.

The Role of the Sales Manager

The sales manager's role is changing. Effective sales managers will lead by creating an environment that allows people to reach their full potential. The proper vision, effective values and a strong sense of purpose set the tone for leadership and enable the sales culture to flourish. Direction and control are on the way out, and maintaining a sense of balance and order are in. The best leaders are those who do not seek credit for the success of their employees. They lead without managing and manage without control. Effective leaders give their employees accountability and trust. The wise leader will then leave them alone. The leader recognizes that the employee will succeed or fail and that there is more to gain from failure than accomplishment or success. More importantly, individuals will give more and be rewarded in a more valuable way when given freedom and empowerment.

Team Selling

The sales team is changing as reps work together in synergy to create a strong sales organization. Sales people realize the importance of the entire company being successful and reaching financial objectives. Sales teams use a team-selling approach to maximize each other's strengths and better meet customer's needs. The team shares the rewards and works together to hit the organization's revenue targets. Those who are stronger at prospecting should focus in that area. Others may be better at qualifying, building relationships and handling the politics of the complex sale. Others may be better suited to closing. They are very comfortable asking for the sale and have strong intuitive abilities to help guide them. This team approach can be very effective to maximizing sales.

Wood-Young Consulting Goals and Objectives

1. Develop Win-Win Client Relationships

- Provide our clients with valuable information that helps them increase revenues.

- Recommend resources and provide solutions to our clients.

• Treat clients as partners and develop strong relationships through trust, hard work and results.

• Provide companies with effective and cost-efficient project development and implementation.

• Bring new, creative, effective, practical ideas to the client.

• Be flexible and provide a wide range of services to meet client needs and add value.

• Compliment the client, be collaborative with them, focus on ROI and set fees based on the return to the client. Guarantee the work to increase sales, modify or stop.

• The risk should be low to the client when compared to the potential returns.

• Emphasize results, not tasks; show how tasks will lead to results and revenues.

2. Results Focused Sales Training

• Provide comprehensive training services focusing in the areas of motivation and sales training. Other areas can be covered at the request of the client. The training is specifically tailored to each client and results in increased employee performance. The programs are practical, results-oriented and motivational. The sales training involves high-quality, facilitated training and consulting sessions for sales professionals of all types, including sales managers, telephone sales reps, field sales and customer service professionals.

• The goals of the program are to provide sales managers and reps with effective sales and motivational training programs that encourage them to improve themselves as professionals. This will result in individual goal attainment. Training programs will be interactive, open discussion forums. They will focus on how the customer can be helped and serviced. The sessions are based on trust and honesty, and how selling and personal development can lead to proven results. The goal is to train and educate sales professionals to improve their job performance and increase their work effectiveness.

- The sessions are discussion-oriented and results-based, with participants doing much of the work.

- At the conclusion of the training sessions, reps should have a thorough understanding of selling in the present and future along with personal action plans. They should be on their way to becoming "Sales Masters."

- Reps will be coached on self-development, sales fundamentals, and how to develop an action plan to get results.

- Focus is on learning and changes in behavior that will lead to positive results.

- Make use of a comprehensive manual for sales training, personal development, marketing, and management.

3. Provide Effective Marketing Consulting Services

- Offer our clients marketing and sales-focused consulting services.

- Be prepared to offer additional management consulting services if needed.

- Facilitate meetings and help customers brainstorm to gain new insights that will improve their business and increase revenues.

- Provide an independent viewpoint and expertise in areas of sales and marketing management and offer creative solutions.

- Constantly explore new technologies and marketing programs to support the client, including e-commerce solutions.

- Offer Internet marketing and Web site development services that develop competitive advantages for clients.

4. Marketing and Sales Project Management

- Provide project management services that are focused on marketing, sales and management initiatives.

- Include plan development, implementation, evaluation and modification.

- Go one step further than other consultants by actually seeing the plan through to completion.

Wood-Young Consulting Sales Training

Sales training programs can be customized to meet the specific needs of the organization, or a standard two-day "Sales Master" workshop can be presented – or a combination of both. The training is designed to improve selling skills and motivate sales professionals to improve continuously. The sales program pulls key, related elements from many types of sales and motivational training and mixes it with sound, time-tested common sense. Prior to the actual training, a planning day is scheduled with key managers to review the objectives of the training, select topics and create the customized training manual that is used in the workshops.

Sales professionals of all abilities and experience will learn from the training. The facilitated workshops allow senior reps to offer their input and the open forum allows for questions from those new to sales.

Sales Training Program Topics

The following areas are discussed openly in facilitated training sessions with the sales reps and managers. A sales and marketing action plan is developed for the sales team and each individual sales rep. The action plan includes the critical steps which enable the sales and marketing training to increase revenues for the sales rep, the team and the organization. Following is a partial list of training topics:

- Traits of Successful Sales People
- Everything Begins with Attitude
- Personal Development as a Sales Professional
- Rewards of Personal Development
- Mission Statement and Goal Setting
- How to Implement Personal Goals and Measure Results
- How to Motivate Yourself Every Day
- Organization and Time Management
- Balance of Mental, Emotional, Spiritual and Physical
- The Power of the Subconscious
- Focus and Persistence
- Prospecting and Lead Generation
- Dealing With Fear in Sales
- Qualifying, Probing Questions and Scripting
- Listening Skills
- Objections

- Presentations that Focus on Benefits
- Closing that is Automatic
- How to Add Value to a Customer
- Relationship Building
- How to Build Trust
- Accessing and Working with Personality Types
- Account-Based Selling
- Selling a Service
- Passion
- How to be Creative and Analytical
- Negotiation Skills
- The Power of the Subconscious
- Why your Customers Buy
- Communication Skills

Professional Telephone Selling

- Why Telephone Selling is Key to Success
- Review the Unique Characteristics of Phone Selling
- Lead Generation and Prospecting on the Phone
- Scripts
- Objections on the Phone
- Probing Questions
- How to get an Appointment
- Follow-up on the Phone
- Telephone Presentations
- Conference Calls
- Voice Mail, Screeners and Gatekeepers
- How to Build a Telephone Relationship
- How to Deal with Telephone Burnout
- Closing Sales on the Telephone

Sales Management and Leadership

- Team Mission Statements
- How to Hire Exceptional Sales People
- Performance Evaluations
- How to Motivate your Reps
- Forecasting and Team Goal Development
- Sales Contents and Special Incentives
- Compensating the Sales Team
- Teamwork in Sales
- Future Sales Trends
- How Will Customers Respond to Personal Selling in the Future?

Self-Development and Motivational Training Sessions

- Personal Mission Statements
- The Employee's Role on the Team
- Goal Development
- How to Implement Personal Goals and Measure Results
- How to Motivate Yourself Every Day
- How Personality Types Impact Teamwork
- Organization and Time Management
- Rewards of Personal Development
- Importance of Positive Thinking
- Balance of Mental, Emotional, Spiritual and Physical
- The Power of the Subconscious
- Focus and Persistence

Personal Sales Action Plan

Each sales rep involved in the training develops a personal action plan that includes a mission statement, goals and objectives, and methods for measuring goals and their impact on the organization. These action plans are forms of commitment to the program and copies should be provided to management for accountability and follow-up (see Chapter 39 for more information).

Worksheet Forms and Exercises

The following worksheets are the tools used to create sales action plans and a part of the training's interactive process. They are completed to organize and support the sales process. These projects are personalized to the needs of the sales team and the organization. Following are a few of the worksheets and exercises from the sales training program:

- Personal Mission Statement and Goals
- Ideal Sales Rep Worksheet
- Sales Action Plan
- How to Improve Attitude
- Personal Assessment Worksheet: Opportunities, Threats, Strengths, Weaknesses and Personality
- Target Market Worksheet
- Prospecting and Lead Generation Worksheet and Exercise
- Dealing with Fear in Sales
- Customer Profile
- Features/Benefits
- Probing Questions Worksheet
- Customer Objections
- 30-Second Commercial
- Personal Sales Tracking
- How Does Your Product/Service Add Value?
- How to Build Trust
- Competitive Analysis
- Personality Exercise
- Telephone Selling Script Development

- Why your Customers Buy
- Trial Closes and Closing Statements

Role Playing

Role playing during sales training is a critical element and the first step toward changing behaviors and improving selling skills. Each area in the training can be set up for role playing exercises. This is discussed in the planning meetings with managers.

Sales training provides sales professionals with practical, time-tested solutions that work. Successful sales people act upon this information and close more sales. Feel free to contact individuals who have benefited from Wood-Young sales training.

Why Hire Outside Consultants and Trainers?

Following are the top 10 reasons to contract an outside consultant to train your sales team.

1. Results

Giving sales reps cutting edge, customized selling tools will help maximize production and lead to increased sales. Outside consultants and trainers bring a wealth of valuable information, based on the variety of training and consulting experiences with other organizations. Is your in-house sales training getting results?

2. Buy-In

An outside trainer can better achieve buy-in from the sales team. The outside trainer is a resource for the sales team that is removed from the organizational environment and can help the team achieve goals and objectives. Do you have buy-in from the sales team regarding your current sales training?

3. Saves Money

Training the sales team can be expensive, whether it is in-house or with the aid of an outside consultant. The key is Return on Investment (ROI). Are you getting the maximum ROI from in-house sales training?

4. Saves Time

Bringing the sales team into a training session must be time-effective. The reps are not selling when they are in training. Are your reps maximizing their time in sales training meetings?

5. Keep it Positive

Any time a group of sales people comes together in one room venting and negativity can run rampant. An outside sales trainer will not function as a venting platform for sales reps. Are your training sessions productive and positive, or negative and stressful?

6. Motivational

Outside consultants have learned from years of experience what common training methods actually motivate sales reps. Are your reps highly motivated following sales training sessions?

7. Offer New Perspective

Outside consultants offer new perspectives and view the company from the outside, rather than the often times limiting view of those on the inside of the organization. Does the in-house sales training push reps beyond their comfort zones?

8. Express Value

The outside consultant offers direct value to the sales reps by showing them how to improve themselves and get better sales results. This comes with no strings attached to organizational issues. The trainer is available for follow-up questions. Does company culture, politics or rep performance issues impact your sales training?

9. Create an Educational Environment

The outside trainer creates an atmosphere of learning because he or she is not an official part of the organization and the objective is personal growth and development. Are your training sessions highly productive, learning events?

10. Reach a Win-Win

An outside sales trainer can be a win-win for everyone involved as reps understand and buy in to the fact that success for the company equals success for them. Do your sales reps see in-house sales training as a win-win situation?

Action Step:

1. **For more information on Wood–Young Consulting's sales training programs and consulting services, visit www.SalesTrainingPlus.com.**

List of Great Books

Byrd Baggett
The Book of Excellence, Rutlidge Hill Press

Harry Beckwith
Selling the Invisible, Warner Books

E. Thomas Behr
The Tao of Sales, Element

Robert Bly
Secrets of Successful Telephone Selling, Owl Books

Lee Boyan
Successful Cold Call Selling, Amacom

Jack Carew
The Mentor, Plume

Richard Carlson
Don't Worry Make Money, Hyperion
Don't Sweat the Small Stuff at Work, Hyperion
Don't Sweat the Small Stuff, Hyperion

Lynea Corson, George Hadley & Carl Stevens
The Secrets of Super Selling, Berkeley

Stephen Covey
First Things First, Fireside
The 7 Habits of Highly Effective People, Fireside

Kevin Daley
Socratic Selling, McGraw-Hill

Lawrence Friedman and Timothy Furey
The Channel Advantage, Butterworth Heinemann

Gene Garofalo
Sales Managers' Desk Book, 2nd Ed., Prentice Hall

Saul W. Gellerman
Motivation in the Real World, Plume

Barbara Geraghty
Visionary Selling, Simon and Schuster

Jeffrey Gitomer & Ron Zemke
Knock Your Socks Off Selling, Amacom

Gary Grikscheit
Handbook of Selling, John Wiley

Stephen Heiman & Diane Sanchez
The New Strategic Selling, Warner Books

Bruce Hyland & Merle Yost
Reflections for Managers, McGraw-Hill

Ron Kerr
The Titan Principle, Chandler House Press

Otto Kroeger and Janet Thuesen
Type Talk at Work, Dell Books

Roger C. Parker
Relationship Marketing on the Internet, Streetwise

James Porterfield
Teleselling, John Wiley

Neil Rackham
SPIN Selling, McGraw-Hill

Al Ries and Laura Ries
The 11 Immutable Laws of Internet Branding, Harper Business

Susan Roane
How to Work a Room, Warner Books

W.G. Ryckman
Compensating Your Sales Force, Probus

David Sandler and John Hayes
You Can't Teach a Kid to Ride a Bike at a Seminar, Dutton

Stephan Schiffman
High Efficiency Selling, John Wiley

Brian Tracy
Advanced Selling Strategies, Fireside

Paco Underhill
Why We Buy: The Science of Shopping, Simon and Schuster

List of Great Web Sites, Magazines, Newspapers, Newsletters and Other Resources

The resources listed below can help you learn more about sales and stay updated on the current trends. The amount of information available is enormous and overwhelming. I have taken the time to research a few of the best resources. Visit them often, stay informed and add more value to your customers.

Sales and marketing sites that are loaded with information:

www.JustSell.com
www.SalesBureau.com
www.SalesLobby.com
www.Sales.com
www.SalesRepCentral.com
www.Gitomer.com
www.HeadquarterSales.com
www.SalesGuy.com
www.SalesDoctors.com
www.SalesTrainingPlus.com

Internet marketing sites and other Web resources:

www.ClickZ.com
www.Internet.com
www.SuperStats.com
www.SearchEngineWatch.com
www.KeyWordCount.com
www.Goto.com
www.WordTracker.com
www.Forrester.com
www.gsbc.com
www.Gartner.com
www.cnn.com
www.1stPosition.com
www.TheStandard.com

www.emarketer.com
www.UseIt.com
www.WebPositionGold.com
www.WoodYoungConsulting.com

List and lead databases:

Info USA
www.InfoUSA.com

Dun and Bradstreet
www.dnb.com

Top sales and marketing magazines and newspapers:

Selling Power
www.SellingPower.com

Sales and Marketing Management
www.SalesandMarketing.com

Revolution
www.RevolutionMagazine.com

Time Digital
www.TimeDigital.com

Business2.0
www.Business2.com

Wall Street Journal
www.wsj.com

Newsletters:

The Economics Press Inc.
www.epinc.com
Dynamic Selling
SalesMasterMind
Customer Service
And more...

Briefing Publishing Group
www.combriefings.com
The Competitive Advantage
Team Management Briefings
Communication Briefings
And more...

Bureau of Business Practice
www.bbpnews.com
Professional Selling
Strategic Sales Management
And more...

Clement Communications
www.Clement.com
Master Salesmanship
And more...

Dartnell Corporation
www.DartnellCorp.com
Sales and Marketing
Handling Objections
Sales Leader
Successful Closing Techniques
Prospecting
Selling
Motivated to Sell
And more...

Index

ego 22, 23, 24, 25, 27, 75, 87, 205
email 58, 95, 99, 100, 181, 189, 194, 204
emotional 3, 15, 16, 17, 21, 34, 56, 65, 67, 70, 71, 83, 85, 86, 113, 131, 140, 143, 146, 147, 148, 149, 164, 165, 222, 224
emotions 16, 17, 29, 68, 70, 71, 83, 84, 85, 117, 140, 143, 148, 165, 217
end-user 125, 126, 128
environment 17, 20, 23, 37, 38, 102, 103, 104, 106, 174, 204, 215, 216, 217, 226, 228
equipment 102
ethics 155, 204
exercise 15, 225, 226
extraverts 141, 142

F
face-to-face 99, 125
facilitated training 219, 222
fax 58, 99, 100
fear 19, 24, 33, 56, 57, 62, 63, 64, 65, 76, 132, 134, 151, 153, 157, 158, 165, 178, 198, 223, 226
features 110, 186, 225
feedback 19, 38, 42, 75, 76, 93, 118, 122, 126, 132, 183, 192, 194
feel, felt, found 86, 87
feeling 16, 56, 63, 72, 83, 114, 131, 132, 140, 141, 142, 143, 146, 165
first impression 57, 108, 111
flash 181
focus 12, 18, 19, 26, 29, 32, 33, 34, 36, 37, 40, 41, 50, 51, 54, 55, 56, 68, 75, 77, 80, 99, 102, 109, 117, 118, 122, 143, 144, 148, 152, 158, 165, 181, 190, 194, 195, 199, 203, 205, 209, 214, 217, 218, 219, 220, 222, 224
follow-up 58, 59, 99, 102, 104, 107, 113, 186, 223, 225, 228
follow-up activities 57

G
gatekeepers 98, 100, 223
Goldmine Software 57, 100
government 54, 181

H
Heinman, Stephen 124, 231
hits 180, 184, 190
homework 42, 55, 117, 121

About the Author

Thomas Wood-Young is a writer, consultant and sales trainer. He is the president of Wood-Young Consulting, a marketing consulting firm. Tom has more than 16 years of experience in sales and marketing, spanning his entire professional career, as both a sales rep and manager. He realized the importance of personal selling when he owned his first business at 24 years old. This led to a career in sales and a burning desire to help companies and sales teams succeed. Tom has a BA in communications from the University of Northern Colorado and an MBA from the University of Colorado at Colorado Springs. He was a collegiate swimmer, triathlete and currently an avid tennis player.

Tom has had the opportunity to work with thousands of sales people, providing sales training services, recruiting, motivation, team building and helping them perform at top levels. He has consulted with a diverse group of companies across the country, including NEC, Harcourt, PaperDirect, The American Funds, EAS, and Spyderco, to name a few. Tom is an adjunct instructor of management and marketing at the University of Phoenix, a keynote speaker and has been featured in numerous publications and Web sites.

He has led on-line seminars on the CompuServe Sales Forum; conducted public seminars on sales, marketing, and Web site strategies; and a has been a guest on "Hot Talk," the Business-of-Business radio program. He writes a monthly marketing and sales column for *InBIZ*.

Tom lives in Colorado Springs, Colo., with his two children, Bryce and Blake, and his wife, Pamela.